C.A. MEIER

PERSONALITY

Natura infinita est
sed qui symbola animadverterit
omnia intelliget
licet non omnino

C.A. Meier

Personality

The Individuation Process
in Light of C.G. Jung's Typology

Translated by David N. Roscoe

DAIMON

Title of the original German edition: *Persönlichkeit*,
© 1977 Walter-Verlag

The author and the publisher gratefully acknowledge the generous assistance of Mrs. Joyce Ashley and the Ann and Erlo von Waveren Foundation in making this publication possible.

Library of Congress Cataloging in Publication Data

Meier, C.A. (Carl Alfred), 1905–
    Personality.

    (The Psychology of C.G. Jung, v. 4)
    Translation of: Persönlichkeit
    Bibliography: p. 175
    Index: p. 183
    1. Personality.   2. Jung, C.G. (Carl Gustav), 1875-1961   3. Typology
II. Series: Meier, C.A. (Carl Alfred), 1905–
Lehrbuch der Komplexen Psychologie C.G. Jungs.
English; v. 4.

ISBN 3-85630-549-1 (paper)
ISBN 3-85630-551-3 (hardcover)

© 1995 Daimon, Einsiedeln, Switzerland
cover photo: Buddhist Temple at Borobudur, Java, 8-9th cent.
Photograph of the author by Sam Francis

Contents

In memoriam C.G. Jung
Centum Annorum
1875–1975 A.D.
Knowledge is the specific nature of the Psyche.
Corpus Hermeticum X, 9

Acknowledgments

Except where otherwise noted, translations of source material are by David Roscoe. All English citations of C.G. Jung are drawn from his Collected Works, Bollingen Series XX, Princeton: Princeton University Press. All Faust passages, again, unless otherwise noted, are drawn from the George Madison Priest translation.

The use of the following illustrations is gratefully acknowledged: "O Great Eye" from Loka: A Journal from Naropa Institute published by Anchor Press/Doubleday, New York. "The Aristotelian Concept of the Four Humors" from Astrology, the Celestial Mirror, published by Thames and Hudson, London, and Avon Books, New York. "Ophion and the Universal Egg," "The Sefiroth Depicted as the Androgynous Adam Kadmon," "The Kabbalistic Tree of Life," "The Sefiroth as the Tree Pillars," and "The Path of Kundalini" from Kabbalah, copyright © 1973 by Charles Poncé, published by Straight Arrow Books. "Abraxas" from A Fantastic Bestiary published by Leon Amiel Publishers, New York. "The Taoist Form of Internal Alchemy" British Museum. The chart for "Two Modes of Consciousness" from The Psychology of Consciousness by Robert E. Ornstein Published by W.H. Freeman and Company, San Francisco. Copyright © 1972.

The quotation from "East Coker" in Four Quartets by T.S. Eliot is reprinted with permission from Harcourt Brace Jovanovich, Inc., New York, and Faber & Faber, Ltd., London.

Preface

The aim of this last volume of our textbook series on "complex Psychology," is to deal with the purpose and meaning of all individual psychological endeavor in the Jungian sense of the term. Jung, as is commonly known, coined the term individuation to describe the objective of this conflict between the conscious and the unconscious. The objective itself, however, will only be dealt with indirectly or in symbolic terms. What we *shall do* is attempt to outline the *path* to individuation, because the objective itself is an extrapolation which usually only becomes apparent in symbolic form, if at all. Mindful of Jung's statement that in the bewildering variety of experience with so many different kinds of people, he would be loath to dispense with the compass of typology, we shall embark on what will be the first attempt to describe this individuation path or process, using this typological schema as our guide.

This will be a theoretical representation but will be based on extensive clinical experience. We have largely dispensed with casuistic description, for it often turns out to be misleading. This can be seen in what have become classical examples of this kind, such as the two detailed case descriptions in *Mythology of the Soul* by H.G. Baynes (London 1940), which turned out to be inaccurate. Both patients, contrary to predictions, later developed quite normally and became successful, creative people. Until a patient has died, not even analysts are in a position to have an overview and pass judgement on his development process up to his natural end. Fortunately for the two cases concerned, medical prediction is inaccurate when it comes to the workings of destiny! What is more, there is an adequate supply of literature on the subject of casuistics, in the broadest sense of the term, although these days it is often somewhat lacking in taste.

There is another reason for our choosing the typological schema as the basis of our representation of the psychic processes: the preponderance of one attitude (introverted or extroverted) or one function (Thinking, Feeling, Sensation, Intuition) in one person, and the opposite in another person, forms the basis for much misunderstanding and intolerance, but also for love and hate, war and peace. In other words, the preponderance of attitudes is the basis for the most intimate, as well as the most collective dynamic processes of our souls, and often has disastrous consequences, which could be mitigated, if not averted, if we were more aware of the differences between people in terms of their *typological condition*. This perspective then leads to an attenuation of the effects, as well as to a greater tolerance of others. Unfortunately, this last attitude usually comes about only with advanced age, i.e., *on a physiological* level, when we have already committed our worst deeds and can only forget them thanks to charitable *physiological* amnesia. In contrast, Jung, with his typology, attempts on a psychological level to do justice to these interesting but often irritating differences between people. He does so while we are still involved in life, before the mellowness of old age has made opposites less of a thorn in the flesh.

Since Freud and Jung, the conflict between the conscious and the unconscious has been described in terms of dynamic psychology, and with E. Bleuler it has been referred to as depth psychology. Those who have scant respect for these theories will derive little benefit from reading this book. But those who see themselves as "being on track" may occasionally gain from applying the Jungian compass. They will see whether or not the typological theory discussed in the third volume of this textbook series can prove its worth in life. The abstraction at the basis of our attempt actually comes from observing life, and should thus take on flesh and blood in the life of every individual.

"On then with the task!"

Chapter I

The Typological Schema

A. Introduction

The third volume of this textbook series (*Consciousness,* 1989), dealt with the phenomenology of consciousness. In doing this, we brought in C.G. Jung's psychological typology, but touched only lightly here and there on the dynamics that derive therefrom. This was most clearly apparent toward the end of the book, where we attempted to summarize in seven fundamental sentences the laws arising from this typology. The opposing positions in the psyche, which are traced back to their psychological elements, always imply tensions that can vent themselves in violent movements and can confront people with crucial problems. As promised in the Preface, this volume will demonstrate these psychological dynamics under the aspect of the different typical attitudes people have; it is hoped that the application of the typology will help us bring a certain order to these phenomena.

At this point, however, we must make a preliminary comment and state certain reservations. Whenever the subject of dynamics crops up in psychology, there usually arise automatic associations to much-used model concepts from the field of physics. Ever since Freud, there have been attempts in psychology, and especially in analytical psychology, to adopt the terminology of physics to understand the essence and functioning of the libido. Libido was defined as sexual or psychic energy, leading to lots of borrowings from the field of thermodynamics. In Volume 3 of this textbook series, we objected to such misleading forms of expression. There should be no attempt to deny phenomenological parallels, but here and now we should like to warn against understanding psychological constructs in terms of the natural sciences. In the psychic sphere, libido, content, and further compounds and derivatives, such as empathy and even entropy, can only describe the determinable valency of the aforementioned external (empathy) or internal object. One could speak of consciousness as a potential, or level. But this always involves an evaluation. In physics there is no room for values, since they are a purely psychic phenomenon, with the result that our borrowings inevitably remain a pathetic reduction and the specifically psychic aspect is examined out of existence. As early as 1935,[1] we pointed out the convergences in terminology between physics and psychology, but the reasons for this go much deeper than the physicalistic libido theories would have us superficially believe. The deeper experimental physics goes into the inside of matter, which cannot be apprehended in sensory terms, the more clearly we see in its definitions and concepts symbolic forms of expression which, in turn, reveal an extremely curious analogy to the findings of the psychology of the unconscious. So when psychologists feel provoked and apply their *déformation professionnelle* to seek an understanding of this curious convergence, they are not only entitled to do so but actually find it necessary. For here we are at the very point where physics and psyche come together, and this is probably one of the greatest puzzles to confront mankind.

The valency of psychic contents or concepts is, in most cases, known to us, but their dimensions are far from being measurable in the way that physical dimensions are. We can ascertain that something strikes us as particularly interesting and provides us with strong motivation or impetus, and that we have a preference for, or inclination toward, a certain thing. We can also consciously ascertain the opposite phenomena, Such as resistance, aversion or lack of impetus. The term that most easily comes to mind for this is *potential.* In a manner of speaking, a specific psychic content has at its disposal a high or low potential, which is simply another term for its *valency.*

A purely *formal* approach to observing psychic contents obviously dispenses with this aspect and hence leads to little more than a sort of taxonomy or classification. This, too, can be of interest, particularly if it results in a hierarchy of the concepts, but calls for a vast amount of statistical material. On the other hand, as early as the beginning of this century, Freud discovered what happens to the contents of the psyche

---

[1] C.A. Meier, "Moderne Physik – moderne Psychology," in *Die kulturelle Bedeutung der Komplexen Psychologie*, Festschrift on the occasion of the 60th birthday of C.G. Jung, Berlin 1935, pp. 349-362, now also in: C.A. Meier, *Experiment und Symbol*, Olten 1975, pp. 9-18.

when, for example, a specific inclination gives way to lack of interest, i.e., using the terms of reference mentioned above, when a content has lost its potential. He was able to prove that such a drop in potential affected only the capacity of the content of consciousness. As regards the content, there was no actual loss in formal terms. The forgotten or suppressed contents could be traced back to the unconscious. In other words, all that had happened was a displacement in the consciousness/ unconsciousness system.

We have given instances of such displacement in Volume 1 of this textbook series. Here, too, the question arises as to whether it is particularly meaningful to observe such a phase change from an energetic point of view. If we want a systematic representation, there is more to be gained by viewing the psyche as a "self-regulating system." This term has proved valuable in the field of biology and, with the necessary changes, should also have value in the field of psychology. At any rate, a) the correlation of consciousness with the external world can easily be viewed from this angle, in that the sensory-physiological aspect belongs totally to the biological sphere. The relation b) consciousness/body can also be seen as self-regulating, the obvious example being in the case of hunger. We are now on the very border between the environment and the inner world, and here it is not so easy to demonstrate self-regulation, despite the promising statements formulated by J. v. Uexküll[2] back in 1921. What is even more difficult to prove is c) the self-regulating relation consciousness/unconsciousness, for the simple reason that it is not really possible to conduct further experiments here. In this respect we are almost exclusively dependent on clinical observation, for psychic disturbances can be viewed for this purpose as experiments set up by Nature. Also, from a historical point of view it was the clinic that first had grounds for understanding the nature of this relation as self-regulating. In psychic *disturbances,* in particular, it can be seen clearly that the normally automatically functioning regulating mechanism has failed. But even in cases of good health, the cooperation between consciousness and unconsciousness is not always successful, as we can see readily in ourselves if we think about it. We need only recall Romans 7:18-19: "for to will is present

[2]J. v. Uexküll, *Umwelt und Innenwelt der Tiere.* 2nd ed., Berlin 1921; id., *Theoretische Biologie*, 2nd ed., Berlin 1928.

with me, but to do that which is good is not. For the good which I would I do not: but the evil which I would not, that I practice."

We, too, feel the way St. Paul did, and we feel sure that Parmenides was talking about this same conflict when he described people as two-headed without regarding it as an illness.[3] But this inadequate coopera-tion between consciousness and unconsciousness is felt as very unsatis-factory, obviously because it indicates a disturbance in the self-regulat-ing system. Some people can accept this state of affairs, but others feel the need to seek help, from a psychologist, for example. The task is then to rectify the disturbance in the regulating system. Ever since Freud and Jung, the procedure for this has been to take into account the contents of the unconscious that are parallel or anti-parallel to the conscious and thus be in a position to restore the missing or inadequate cooperation between the two systems. What emerges from this is the knowledge that good health corresponds to the perfect functioning of the self-regula-tion. And now, using Jung's working hypothesis of typology, we shall show how this relation of consciousness/unconsciousness manifests itself in the sense of a healthy development of the personality.

In the third volume of this textbook series we described Jung's typological argument in greater detail. For that reason we shall give a brief summary of it here; it will serve as the basis of our further remarks.

B. Recapitulation of Jung's Typology

1. The four functions

Jung distinguishes four formal basic or orienting functions of con-sciousness. His idea is to apprehend the most elementary instruments of consciousness, which cannot be further analyzed or reduced. They are thus very easily defined in comparison to the countless other character-istics of consciousness, which are at once both more complex and more complicated. He distinguishes sensation (S), thinking (T), feeling (F), and intuition (I). These functions make possible the following statement about a content of consciousness that must be dealt with:

[3] Parmenides, fr. B6, 5.

1st Fundamental principle

The S is *that something* exists, and *how* it is made;
The T is *what it* is and what it means;
The F is what its *value is to* me; and
The I is its *possibilities,* such as whence it comes and whither it goes.

2nd Fundamental principle

These four functions can be divided into two pairs, in that T and F are discriminative and rational, whereas S and I are perceiving and irrational.

3rd Fundamental principle

Within the individual pair the two functions are in opposition to each other (e.g., anyone who feels cannot simultaneously think, and vice-versa). In other words, the functions are mutually exclusive.

4th Fundamental principle

So one can say that someone is a thinker, someone else a feeling type, i.e., one orients himself preferably with the thinking function, the other preferably according to his feelings. This main function is his strong point, works reliably, and is thus referred to as the differentiated, or simply, the main function. On the basis of the principle of exclusion the other function can be assumed to function weakly in comparison, which is why we refer to it as the inferior function. The other two functions have a sort of intermediate position.

Because of the opposition or exclusion relationship, Jung felt he had proven that the inferior function is largely excluded from consciousness and thus exists in the sphere of the unconscious, where it can make its presence felt only indirectly and by means of rather peculiar effects.

2. The two attitudes

The starting point for Jung's typology was the fact that people usually have a preference for one specific "intellectual talent" and exploit it to the full. The second point was the observation that the relevant function (main function) takes its place in a general reference system in different ways. There are a *priori* two different possibilities:

The main function is related mainly a) internally, to the ego, or mainly b) externally, to the outside world.

Depending on which way the interest of the main function flows, Jung talks of introversion in the case of a), and in the case of b) of extroversion. Whether one's attitude follows a) or b) is decided by an aprioristic *value accent,* which has all the qualities of the numinous. For introversion the reference system is the subject and its connection with his inner world and also with the unconscious side. For extroversion the reference system is the object and the relation of the subject with the outside world.

In Volume 3 of this textbook series we gave a long list of external manifestations by which the two attitude types are distinguished. In this volume we shall attempt to understand how *internal situations* correspond to these external characteristics, of which we shall give a brief selection here.

a) *introverted*   b) *extroverted*

1. rejection of external influence   1. complaisance

2. timid, cautious   2. trusting

3. cold   3. warm

4. unfriendly   4. friendly

5. critical   5. enthusiastic

6. pessimistic   6. optimistic

7. persistent   7. erratic

8. apathetic   8. impulsive

9. haughty   9. willing to reveal oneself

10. miserly   10. extravagant

11. rigid mimicry   11. flexible mimicry

12. a poor mixer   12. a good mixer

13. individualism   13. collectivism

Now we shall look at the significance these characteristics have for the individual. We must bear in mind, however, that the person concerned is usually totally unaware of this significance.

Let us begin by looking at the significance of certain external phenomena for the individual with the *introverted* attitude. It is easy to see that the listed characteristics 1-4 and 11-12, which manifest themselves externally, may be attributed to the person's great sensitivity. He is "thin-skinned" and so the impressions that come at him from all sides strike deep and affect him greatly. He seeks to protect himself through characteristics 1-4 and 11-12, and in a way they help maintain his self-preservation.

The psychiatrist Otto Gross has created a very graphic model for this situation, which of course we shall not take literally.[4] He talks of a "cerebral secondary function," by which he simply means the restitution phase of a stimulated nerve cell. The absorption of the stimulus would be the primary function. Only when the "secondary function" subsides is the cell once again in a position to absorb a new stimulus, so that newly occurring stimuli cannot even be perceived during the secondary function. Gross postulates that some people are born with a prolonged secondary function. This would be a very apt description of the type described by Jung as *introverted,* and we could depict it in graphic terms: his primary function is strong, even violent, as there is a lot of tension there which usually betrays itself, for example, in his rigid mimicry. To recover from this he consequently needs a longer restitution phase, described by Gross as a "prolonged secondary phase." Of course, several new stimuli fall into this phase, but during this extension they have no effect (Figure 1).

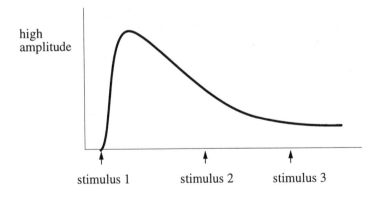

Figure 1. Prolonged secondary function

---

[4] Otto Gross, *Die cerebrale Sekundärfunktion*, Leipzig 1902; id., *Über psychopathische Minderwertigkeiten*, Leipzig 1909.

This gives rise to a surfeit of stimuli, which in turn leads to a flight from stimuli. For the same reason, the introverted type tends to miss the right opportunities and suffer from *esprit d'escalier*. This is connected with the fact that this attitude type is vindictive, which is also why the introvert is afraid of his own emotions and is envious and jealous of the extroverted type, who seems to have a much easier time of it. In other words, he secretly yearns for extroversion. Another distinguishing feature is a certain slowness in forming *his own opinion,* even though there is actually a strong need for this on his part.

On the other hand, it is precisely for the above reasons that the introverted type has considerable awareness of his motives and is very self-critical, which often gives rise to the so-called inferiority complexes. The introvert is generally full of himself and this is why he comes across as reserved. The overvaluation of the object, and the fascination with it, force him to defend himself against it. He acts basically according to the "subjective factor" (cf. pp. 71-72 of Volume 3), and this makes his consciousness a subjective one.

We shall now attempt to make the same examination of the inner equivalent of the external manifestations of the extroverted type. The listed characteristics of the extrovert that manifest themselves externally, 3-6 and 8-9, correspond to "inner truths," to the fact that he is "thick-skinned" and that influences on him do not go very deep; on the contrary, stimuli have little effect on him and there is an inner coldness. He keeps a safe distance from the object.

With Otto Gross one would have to speak of a "shortened secondary function" giving rise to a hunger for stimuli. The "amplitude" of the "primary function" is not high, given the lower tension, and with the extrovert the lower tension reveals itself externally in his relaxed mimicry (cf. Figure 2).

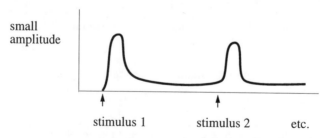

small
amplitude

stimulus 1   stimulus 2   etc.

Figure 2. Shortened secondary function.

The extroverted type has no great need to form his own opinion, because this is replaced by the large number of perceived stimuli, which, to a certain extent, amount to an externally *given* opinion. The extrovert's own emotions are something he takes for granted and he never fully realizes what his own motives are. This is why he is unable to be self-critical and tends to be high-handed and pompous. Because he has an inadequate feeling relationship to the object, he usually underestimates it and this in turn tempts him to flee into the outside world. Whereas the introvert tends to shut himself up with his dominating complex, the extrovert energetically blocks it out. Through extensive adjustment to the objective he is lost to the environment and gets caught up in it. This means that he hardly perceives his inner world and sees it as predominantly negative in the object world (via projection, a subject to which we shall return shortly).

Thus a psychology geared to extroversion is based mainly on objectivity and causality. The most general things will be regarded as the truly valid and everything will be reduced to that. This is why Jung understood Freud's psychology from this extroverted point of view. The introvert, on the other hand, will relate essentially to the "subjective factor" and will thus prefer a psychology corresponding to that of Alfred Adler. So each mode of observation is determined by its own attitude type, and if Freud has such a strong influence in the modern world, this is probably because extroversion is so highly regarded in the West. The typological principle enables us thus to do justice to both Freud and Adler and to make proper use of their forms of therapy.

In our earlier examination of the background of the introverted and the extroverted attitude types, we discovered something that corresponds to Jung's typological argument, in accordance with our 5th and 6th fundamental principles: the *internal opposite type* always remains relatively unconscious. This is what gives it its relative inferiority and also its autonomous, i.e., spontaneous, functioning. In this context it should be recalled once again that for the corresponding type either the outside or the inside carries the "numinal accent" *a priori, a* fact which absolutely cannot be reduced to more elementary data.

The existence of this internal, unconscious opposite type is proven first and foremost in its *projection,* because contents of the unconscious are first experienced only in the projection. As the term *projection* will be an important one in all that follows, it would be as well to give a brief definition of it at this point. (C.G. Jung gives a detailed description of it

in Chapter XI, Definition No. 43 of *Psychological Types*). Those
characteristics I do not see or acknowledge as my own, but which are
nevertheless present in my system (in other words, of which I am not
conscious), are the very ones I unfailingly feel I can shrewdly perceive
in my neighbor and can sharply criticize. A classical example of this is
the quotation from the Bible: "Why beholdest thou the mote that is in
thy brother's eye, but considerest not the beam that is in thine own
eye?" (Matthew 7:3 and Luke 6:41-42). So a content is thrown out
(projected) of my system and attached to a more or less innocent party.
It is essential to understand that this process is totally unconscious, so
that a projection is simply there as an established view and cannot be
rectified without painstaking effort of moral will. There is no end to
what one can inflict on others in this way. One must not underestimate
the full significance of the false impressions of my partner that I take
into a relationship. The *tort moral* can have horrendous effects. Yet it
must be said that such projections are not totally groundless, for my
weaknesses are unlikely to be unique. The bearer of the projection has
probably been selected on the basis of a "secret" principle of similarity;
in other words, a hook on which I can hang the projected image must be
present.

There can be no doubt that projections exert an objective effect on
their bearer, thus increasing the moral responsibility involved. However, the mechanism of such a "transference" is highly controversial. Its
effect is particularly clear in *active* projections, i.e., in which this
mechanism is more or less consciously applied, often with the intention
of having a desired effect on the bearer. The process is often a grotesque
one, especially when it goes on as a "participation mystique," between
man and animal (dog and master). Active projections also play a role in
all magic procedures, where a physical effect is actually a precondition
(cf. Chapter IX). In any event, it should be clear that as the opposite type
remains in our unconscious, we regularly project it onto a "suitable"
other, i.e., we feel that it exists in the other where we first perceive it.
We shall now attempt to describe the typical, in this case the typological, projections of this kind.

The introvert will project his opposite type onto an extrovert. He will
judge him as if he had done all those things that he rejects in himself out
of self-criticism, and moreover will attribute bad motives to him.
Naively enough, the introvert regards extroversion in the extrovert as
simply negative. It can *happen* to the introvert that he, too, occasionally

produces extroverted characteristics (i.e. that his unconscious breaks through once in a while), and when that happens they turn out to be *inferior* and often rather ridiculous. In such moments the introvert tends to overestimate the object uncritically and to become fascinated and carried away by it. This leads to his involvement with all sorts of unworthy people and questionable things. His behavior becomes very unusual, he misplaces his trust and exposes himself. The inner center emerges surprisingly from behind the tough exterior, and this center is determinable to the point of weakness. He lapses into sentimental relationships, places impossible expectations on the object and can fall jealously in love. This means, of course, that he has high ideals of friendship and love and is correspondingly disappointed.

This temporary reversal of type, in which the opposite type emerges as inferior, can be seen clearly when the introvert is under the influence of alcohol, completely forgets himself, and would happily launch into the triumphant chorus at the end of Beethoven's Ninth. In a Swiss "Weltspiegel" dating back to 1624 we can read that "many people don't have a good word for anyone unless they are drunk," an observation which is well and truly confirmed by the introversion that predominates in Switzerland.

The extrovert will project his own thick skin onto the introvert, interpreting it as unapproachability, coldness, arrogance, self-interest and egoism. When the "introverted" characteristics *happen to him*, the following picture will emerge: autoeroticism, doubts about the community, resistance to influence, fear of the collective, depressive psychosis, feelings of loneliness (being closed up with the complex), nihilism. He then avoids anything unpleasant, but suffers from childish insecurity. In a man this can lead to temporary impotence, for he is full of sexual fantasies and yet is frightened of sexuality. Similarly, in a woman there can be temporary frigidity. Further manifestations of the inferior opposite type are: destructive self-criticism, meanness, smallmindedness, pedantry and tyranny. In the extrovert, alcohol can lead to depressive and sullen moods or irritability, as well as the notorious "drunken misery."

As can be seen from the above, we have given a clinical view of the *type opposite,* the theory we dealt with at greater length in Volume 3. It may be useful at this point to illustrate Jung's attitude and function typology by means of a diagram (Figure 3, below).

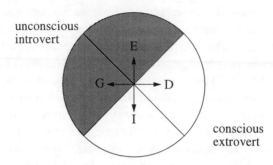

Figure 3. Example of an extroverted intuitive thinking type.

Let us assume that we have with us an extroverted thinking type (T = main function) with intuition (I) as the first auxiliary function. So T and I in his case are in the sphere of the conscious, whereas F and S, in accordance with the principle of exclusion, are dispatched to the unconscious (third fundamental principle). The inferior functions F and S are then active in an inferior way, in line with the idea of the opposite type (sixth fundamental principle). Thus the attitude and function type are coupled together in relation to the opposite type, with the result that the latter is *inferior* both with respect to attitude and function.

In practice, of course, it is not easy to set up a typological diagnosis at first sight. There are all sorts of difficulties involved. It can easily happen that in our neighbor the inferior function is more conspicuous than the superior one, because the main function operates naturally, almost automatically, and thus remains inconspicuous. Furthermore, it is a common human weakness to see another's Achilles heel sooner than his strong points. He presents it to us, if it is important to him, for he has to deal with it constantly to control it as much as possible; otherwise, as can be seen above, he would land in trouble with it. Given the fact that it is so easy to make mistakes, one ought to hold back with a typological diagnosis until the personality is more familiar to us. For this reason it is often easier to make a diagnosis by a process of elimination.

A second difficulty involved in making a diagnosis lies in the fact that in real life we are not dealing with types but with people, and in the human sphere things are always more complicated when it comes to dealing with a scheme or system. In reality there are usually one or two functions that are relatively well differentiated, as in Figure 3. A third function can be fairly well developed too, so that we can speak of a second auxiliary function. Hence the terms main function and first and second auxiliary function have been established. There are in actual fact any amount of combinations.

A third kind of problem consists in the fact that the type can change in the course of life. External influences such as upbringing, family tradition, education, career, the course of one's life and fate can play a role. Their effect can be such that a function (and attitude) that might be of real value can by mischance remain in the dark; an actual "wrong type" can be lived. Just look at all the phoney intellectuals we have today because of the general overestimation of thinking in the Western hemisphere!

It must be emphasized that belonging to one definite type should in no case occasion an argument about ethics, for, as with natural inclination and rejection, the question of guilt does not arise here. Projections onto the opposite type only become reprehensible and dangerous when they occur on a collective basis. The events of the twentieth century bear terrible witness to the effects of mass projections. There is also a collective overestimation of extroversion, and this is not without its dangers: people have little time for introverts, for they do not get involved and so are only reluctantly tolerated. This veneration of the intellect in this day and age also means that the feeling type is misjudged. In summary it can be said that any exaggeration of the type is, because of its one-sidedness, both individually and collectively dangerous and can then become a moral problem.

It is normal that in any individual life there will at some point be a typological turnabout (seventh fundamental principle). Jung refers to this as a *turn of life,* and he attaches a great deal of importance to it. He uses the term *mid-life* for this moment, but it is not something that can be calculated chronologically. There may be biological reasons for this natural reversal, but Jung emphasizes the manifestations involved, for this is what he wants to find out about. Generally these typological changes occur in tiny steps in the course of life, but we usually only become conscious of them at a given moment, i.e. at the turn of life, and they come as somewhat of a surprise to us. In this connection Jung is fond of using the term *enantiodromia,* which means "running counter to." It is said to come from Heraclitus, although it cannot be found in the authentic fragments. However, it does crop up once in the *placita philosophorum* (ed. H. Diels)[5] and it very probably does relate to Heraclitus, for the concept of the naturally transforming of the opposites into each other can be found in several of his Fragments and is a fundamental *tenet* with him.[6]

It would probably be idle speculation to ask whether pre-Socratic philosophy had links with the Far East. However, the indications to be found in Heraclitus bear a striking similarity to Chinese Taoism. *Tao,* the "cosmic order," i.e., the structure and dynamics of the cosmos in the metaphysical sense, is often illustrated there by the famous *Tai-gi-tu* sign (Figure 4).

yang   yin

Figure 4

Tai-gi is reality, as opposed to the possibility *Wu-gi; tu* is the sign which is seen as a mountain with the sun's rays sloping onto it. The red side of the diagram represents the principle of yang, which signifies light, summer, the sun, maleness. The white side signifies yin, darkness, the moon, winter, femaleness. Tao is made up of these pairs of opposites. It can be seen from the *Tai-gi-tu* diagram that at the point where one principle has the greatest extension, the other one is already starting to germinate in the center, i.e. it already bears the seeds of its opposite. In other words, tao is characterized as the dynamic order of opposites connected with each other.

If these two dimensions are to be understood, the following observation must be made: yang signifies a reality that is not spatial but is permanent, light, strong, firm; it represents the positive, the substance and, as a cosmic principle, the creative. Yin, on the other hand, signifies spatial extension, potentiality which is never constant but always changing; it represents the shadowy, the weak, the soft, the negative, the form, and, as a cosmic principle, the receiving.

[5] Placita philosophorum, in Doxographici graeci, I.7, 22 Aëtius, ed. H. Diels, Berlin 1879.
[6] Heraclitus, Fragmenta B 8, 10, 88, 126.

The intensification – we would say the exaggeration – of one opposite gives rise to a movement in the direction of the other, i.e., its transformation. Yang leads to yin and vice-versa. As yang is symbolically represented by a complete stroke and yin by a broken one, the depicted process of the inner transformation of the principles (enantiodromia) can also be illustrated as follows: as, in accordance with its nature, yang expands by movement from the inside to the outside, it has to split up and become yin. As yin, in accordance with its nature, concentrates its movement from outside to inside, it has to unite and become yang.

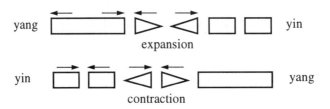

The way these opposites run counter to each other internally obviously contains a time factor, which relates to the typological transformation process as part of the course of life. Normally, of course, it is a process that takes place over a lengthy period of time. There can be no denying that yang and yin show a certain similarity to intro- and extroversion.

It is a well-known fact that the oldest extant oracle book in the world, the Chinese *I Ching* (*Book of Changes*) is based on the principle that opposites change into each other because of their inner dynamic.[7] Its usability is based on the fact that with its help the germ of "becomingness" *(Tai-gi-tu)* can be recognized. If this works, then one is in a position to act accordingly and thus influence the course of the process in its early stages. One is reminded here of the Old Testament prophecies where Heaven reveals ideas which the Saint then turns into a model. Delphi with the Greeks or Praeneste, and the Sibylline books with the Romans can also be seen in this light.

In psychological terms what this turnabout means is simply the emerging into the foreground of the unconscious. As usual, this process

---

[7] *I Ching* (Book of Changes), tr. Wilhelm/Baynes.

can be seen most clearly in psychology in its pathological exaggeration. This can be the result, for example, of too great a rigidity in the original attitude. The change becomes dramatic when it asserts itself unexpectedly and imposes itself as a breakthrough. A well-known case of this is with Nietzsche in his Dionysus experience. In such cases, when the opposite type breaks through it always has regressive-archaic features, since it brings with it elements of the collective unconscious, or, as one usually says, it is contaminated with the collective unconscious. If the original point of view is an extremely rigid one, with an ensuing tentativeness in the change, this can lead to destructive final tendencies, so that instead of a legitimate change there is a radical transformation, a complete overthrow of the original attitude. Everything previously regarded as valid will now be treated with intolerance, fanaticism and cruelty.

The Problem of Opposites

Because the problem of opposites is such a basic and far-reaching fact for our consciousness, it is no surprise that we keep it unconscious for as long as possible. However, because it is also a reality that has an effect, it manifests itself from the unconscious. We saw earlier that what is unconscious usually emerges in projection. The opposite that troubles us will continue to be projected until we understand it better. Initially, however, this projection will take place beyond the human sphere, as far away as possible. As we have just shown, the Chinese gave this problem an agreeable cosmic dimension with yang and yin. Similar forms are found in many mythologies and religions, which we shall look at briefly. To avoid any misunderstandings, let me make it clear that our excursions into the psychology of religion are intended to explain psychology and not religion.

The images serving most clearly to express the problem of opposites are found in the sharply dualistic religions, the oldest representative of which is found in Iran. After the Avesta, Zrvan Akarana (infinitely long duration) has two sons, Ahuramazdah and Ahriman (Middle Persian Ormzud and Angra-mainyn). With the help of the *Ameshaspentas* (light spirits), Ahuramazdah creates the bright world just by being himself in the shining light world. Ahriman opposes every positive creation of the brother with a negative one, in man, too. From the final struggle of the two principles it is Ahuramazdah who emerges victorious. Zarathustra (ca. 550 B.C.) later equated Ahuramazdah with the light principle, announcing his final victory with the aid of the *Saoshyant* (Saviour).

In Egypt there seems to be an analogy to Persia in the two enemy brothers, Osiris (husband of his sister Isis and compared to Dionysus) and Set (the Greek Typhon), the sons of Geb and Nut. Osiris rules Lower Egypt and is responsible for the Nile floodings that bring fertility. Set rules Upper Egypt. He kills his brother Osiris, but is killed in revenge by his own son, Horus. Osiris then becomes ruler in the West Kingdom, Kingdom of the Dead (enantiodromia!).

While we are on the subject of Greece, let us recall the battle of the Titans. Here we find Zeus as the light principle and the god of established world order; opposing him are the Titans, representing the dark principle. They revolt against the order of Zeus, which is why he hurls them into the Tartarus.

With the Germanic peoples, the light principle is represented by Wotan (Scandinavia's Odin), whose dark companion is Loki. His dark side emerges very clearly in his children: Hela, ruler of the underworld, the serpent Midgard and the wolf Fenris. Wotan, on the other hand, is the lord of war and victory. What is more, Loki is an intriguer and, as can be seen with Ragnarök, has a Proteus nature.

The original Persian dualism emerged once again in the 3rd century of our chronology with the Sassanids, with undiminished harshness. Mani (216-277 A.D.) teaches both principles: good, light, god, on the one hand, and evil, darkness, matter on the other. The latter can never ultimately be destroyed. Both principles are mixed together by Satan, which is actually the starting point for cosmogony. Ever since then, the followers of Mani, who lead an ascetic life, have strived to bring together the lost light elements enclosed in the cosmos, which would mean the separating of the two principles and hence redemption. Mani was crucified in 277, but not before Manichaeism had gained a widespread following. The Cathars, or Albigensians, a heretical sect of Christians who were active from the 11th to the 14th centuries, are a later Western form of Manichaeism, both in their teachings and in what happened as a consequence.

We have brought in examples from the history of religion for two reasons: first, to illustrate how the projections of opposites manifest themselves in the history of thought, and second, to show how this can lead to the problem of opposites seemingly remote from earthly man. Moreover, as mentioned earlier, in the Avesta, the Old Iranian sacred writings, there were already initial attempts to take the projected opposite into man, for whenever the god of life and light, Ahura Mazda, creates good in man, his brother, Ahriman, immediately does the opposite. The problem is seen even more clearly in human terms with Mani, for example, where the followers make an active contribution to the world of light by their strict asceticism and their fervent collecting of seeds of light. The classical religions of redemption, such as Buddhism and especially Christianity, pursue this course to its conclusion.

A similar development can be seen in the history of philosophy. This was touched on in Chapter VII of Volume 3 of this textbook series. There we attempted to view from this perspective the history of the dispute about universals, the struggle between the more introverted Realism and the more extroverted Nominalism. Our approach was to start with Plato, proceed via the Megarians and the Cynics to Aristotle, and then to Scholasticism, with its attempts to reconcile faith and reason, showing how they have a common typological background. Let us recall Abelard's attempt at conciliation (p. 81, Volume 3), which was to view the problem in human terms. The problem is fully humanized by Charles François Maria de Rémusat (1797-1875, Paris) in his work on Abelard, when he writes:

> "...between his pure logic and his physics there is a kind of mediatory or halfway science which we may call a psychology;" or later: "his [Abelard's] view is really the modern view in its first form. He heralds it, foretells it, he is its promise."[8]

If we consider these Scholastic speculations as projection, we can draw similar conclusions about contemporary science. We can view the exclusively pure empiricism of modern science, which is confined to causalism, objectivity and reproducibility, as a reversal of Scholastic projection. It is a deep-rooted characteristic of psychologists to regard a specific state as a reaction to an earlier one. The question of whether such an approach would bear fruit with other sciences, such as history, is well worth looking into. A. Toynbee's approach was close to this, as was that of P.A. Sorokine.[9] In a narrower field, such as the history of natural sciences, it would probably be easier to set up such investigations, for they could be carried out using well-defined facts, and it

---

[8] Ch. F.M. de Rémusat, *Abelard*, Paris 1845, 2 vols.
[9] Cf. P.A. Sorokine, *The Crisis of Our Age*, New York 1946.

would be possible to formulate clearly what would be seen as a later reaction to an earlier situation. Apart from Jung's work on alchemy, not much has been done on these lines, although mention must be made of A. Koyré in his *Études Galiléennes I. À l'Aube de la Science Classique,* Paris 1939. In any event, in content a reaction to projection can be seen as compensation, and the reversal process itself can be seen as enantio-dromia.

Chapter II

Phenomenology of the 4 Functions and the 2 Attitudes

To enable us to have an overview of the development of the person-ality, which can be either spontaneous or achieved through analysis, we shall begin with a systematic description of the individual types. This gives us the starting points from which development proceeds. This, of course, presupposes the validity of Jung's theory of the functions, which is still at the experimental stage. We must therefore fall back on clinical observation and at the same time must make a methodical effort to penetrate the prevailing purely empirical experience. The resulting extrapolations, based on an abundance of medical experience with human beings, will prevent us from confusing our description of the types with actual people. This will also keep us aware of the fact that we are conceptualizing, and we advise the reader to bear this in mind as well.

We shall start off with so-called "pure cases." In such cases the problems arising from one-sidedness with regard to the other functions and the opposite attitude are still totally unconscious. This, means that the one-sidedness is often grotesque and provokes corresponding criti-cism from people who are structured differently. But as this criticism in turn is also based on one-sidedness, albeit an opposite one, then it should not imply any moral judgment. On another level, however, the fundamental question arises as to whether the lack of consciousness of a problem should stop it from becoming a moral issue. But this must not be our concern at this point. Our procedure will be to describe the eight different types in the following sequence:

> Extroverted sensation type
> Extroverted thinking type
> Extroverted feeling type
> Extroverted intuitive type

and   Introverted sensation type
Introverted thinking type
Introverted feeling type
Introverted intuitive type.

In each case the description of the main function will be followed by descriptions of the state of the corresponding inferior opposite function and of the phenomena arising from the mixing of the possible auxiliary functions. The inferior opposite function covers almost everything Freud dealt with in great detail under the terms "repression" and "defense mechanisms."

A. *The Phenomenology of the Functions in Extroversion*

1. Extroverted sensation

In recapitulation let us make the general observation that sensation, being an irrational function, does not allow us to make predictions but always conveys only what is given. The numinal accent in this instance lies with the facts, which is why the French expression *fonction du réel* is such an appropriate one. Let us take a brief look at what is meant by "numinal accent:" in coining this phrase, Jung turned to Rudolf Otto, who, in his treatise *Das Heilige,* said that the numinous is one of the main characteristics of the religious experience.[10] According to Otto the numinous combines with the *tremendum* (fear of God), the *stupendum* and the *fascinans* and characterizes the irrational elements of the religious experience. It does not include the ethical content of religion. Otto prefaces his book with the motto, "To feel the thrill of awe crowns man's creation."

The Latin noun *numen* refers originally to the fact that the divinity, perhaps to a person praying before the cult idol, indicates her agreement by inclining her head (nuo, nuere, νεύω). Thus the numinal is a primordial phenomenon. Extroverted sensation, which carries the numinal accent as the main function, perceives the *external* facts and in extreme cases, it is identical with the ego.

[10] Rudolf Otto, *The Idea of the Holy*, Oxford, London, 1923, 1972.

Extroverted sensation as the main function

The extroverted sensation type will always defend today against tomorrow. But come the morrow, this will then be defended against the new tomorrow and so he repeatedly accepts the new situation and takes it for granted. This means that problems are negated almost automatically. The actual psychic factor remains mainly unconscious, so that such types may strike an observer as "people without souls." Fantasy and intuition (as opposite function) are so thoroughly repressed that their very existence is disputed. The possible auxiliary functions (thinking and feeling) are collective in nature and simply coincide with public opinion.

Extroverted sensation types are regarded as objective, down-to-earth people, often largely identified with their careers. They are matter-of-fact and do everything "the way it should be done." They have not the slightest qualms about changing their point of view with a new situation; for them "things are just different now." This means that there are never any feelings of guilt, for they are always in conformity with the facts, little suspecting that there is anything lurking behind these facts. Thus any deviation from the facts would not lead to feelings of guilt. It would be alarming, however, for it would lead to contact with the sphere of irrational possibilities (intuition), i.e., of the unknown, which always arouses apprehension. This brings us to the phenomena of the opposite function in the extroverted sensation type. The opposite function in this case is introverted intuition, which is unconsciously coterminous with the extroverted sensation type. As is always the case with the opposite function, it is only occasionally able to make an appearance, for example, in the form of mistakes, or whenever the conscious attitude is affected by the factors of fatigue or alcohol, when it can break through and cross the threshold of consciousness.

As the main function (S) is extroverted, the opposite function (I) is introverted (5th fundamental principle) and thus produces mainly negative presentiments. Because it is unsound, however, it does not operate on a broad scale as healthy intuition would, but becomes small, narrow and personal. When the opposite function is active, the extroverted sensation type will rise against the facts and attempt to destroy them through distorting fantasies.

When the inferior intuition does break through, quite amazing transformations often result. Let us take a closer look at one example of this: the case of Gustav Theodor Fechner (1801-1887).

After studying medicine, physics and chemistry, he was appointed Professor of Physics in Leipzig. This lasted only until 1840, however, for at the age of 39 Fechner went through a serious crisis, which for three years made it impossible for him to teach. It was a depression, possibly connected with his failing eyesight; in psychiatric terms his condition was defined as a form of manic depression. Fechner confined himself to a room painted black, had his eyes bandaged and took hardly any food. At the end of this "incubation period" his mood turned to hypomania, for he was convinced that he had discovered a universal force as important as Newton's gravity. He called it the "pleasure principle."[11] When he first opened his eyes again in his garden, he "realized" as soon as he looked at the flowers that they had a soul, and he wrote a book with the odd title *Nanna, or The Inner Life of Plants* (1848).

In 1836 Fechner had already published a book, *The Booklet about Life after Death,* whose title hardly suggested that the author was a physicist. This can be seen as a premonitory symptom of an incursion of the inferior function. Similar works followed, such as *Zend Avesta, or The Things of Heaven and the Beyond*[12] (1851) and *The Dayview as opposed to the Nightview* (1879). In the meantime he had exchanged his chair in Physics for one in Philosophy. In 1860 he published his *Elements of Psychophysics,* which can be seen as an attempt to combine his newly acquired intuition with what had previously been exclusively a sensation function. This attempt at synthesis cannot really be counted as successful, even though the law he established, the Weber-Fechner Law, was regarded by W. Wundt as decisively important and laid the foundations for experimental psychology. In any case, Fechner enjoyed good health for the rest of his life.

When the breakthrough came, it was probably all the more violent because of the rather late turn of life. The symptom (failing eyesight) hindered his essentially extroverted optical physical activity (reading instruments) and compelled him to look inwards, i.e., to become introverted. From being a precise, objective, rational natural scientist, he became a "natural philosopher," making highly irrational, subjective speculations.

---

[11] As is commonly known, Freud adopted this term and others from Fechner's "natural philosophy writings."

[12] There is no connection between this and the Zoroastrian Avesta.

Extroverted sensation + Thinking as an auxiliary function

In this type, thinking always remains unconscious to a certain extent, but is nevertheless capable of great achievements. Cooperation with the main function is made easier because of thinking's similar attitude (extroversion). So when an extroverted empiricist possesses a relatively well-differentiated thinking function, the outcome is, for example, an empiricism with systematic reasoning, a way of thinking that is orderly and methodical.

In our opinion, such men as Georges de Cuvier (1769-1832) and Carl von Linné (1701-1778) fall into this category. With the addition of Thinking to his Sensation, Cuvier brought order to the animal kingdom (Le règne animale, 1817) and was the real founder of comparative anatomy. Because of his lack of intuition, however, he opposed Geoffroy St-Hilaire (1772-1844), who was already working on the theory of evolution, which was not compatible with Cuvier's type and only really caught on with Darwin. The dispute between St-Hilaire and Cuvier, which Goethe, too, became involved in, can be seen readily as the result of different typological points of view. In a similar way, Linné created the concise method of naming plants and animals by genus and species, a method which bears his name and is still the basis of modern classification (Systema Naturæ, 1735, and Genera Planatarum, 1737). Because of the addition of Thinking to Sensation, the system is an artificial one; but he also suspects (Intuition) that there must be a natural one as well (an indication of the breakthrough of the opposite).

We can see that this constellation of the functions is bound to produce experts who are not aware of the general significance of their discoveries. As their position in relation to extroversion is a collective one, if they are creative they will not have their own points of view, but will see newly discovered facts only within the framework of the old ones.

Extroverted sensation + Feeling

The addition of feeling to extroverted sensation produces a strong inclination toward the beautiful. That is why this combination is particularly common in art historians or art lovers who are described as aestheticists. In accordance with their extroversion, their point of view remains collective, which is why they can easily adapt to prevailing fashion when it comes to defining beauty. They have no trouble whatsoever in managing to remain "modern."

2. Extroverted thinking

The extroverted thinking type seems to be more commonly found among men. The thinking is discriminating but brings the contents of ideas together in a conceptual relationship. Thinking thus is apperceptive and rational and has a judging function. It enables us to make statements and to pass judgment on a situation or fact. The *numinal accent* rests here on the objective *idea*. In other words, the *quale* of the object is what is important for extroverted thinking. Judgment always presupposes a criterion, however, and this criterion is given by the object or is at least dependent on it. For extroverted thinking, the object is either the objective idea, based on external reality, especially when the auxiliary function is intuition, or it is pure *fact,* when the auxiliary function is sensation.

Extroverted thinking as the main function

In the extrovert, thinking is oriented toward external application, toward objective reality. The extroverted intellect feeds on the object, in a sense, and ultimately leads back to it, thereby excluding the subject. It is a known fact that modern natural science adopts this approach. The prototype of all natural sciences – physics – has forced us to come to terms with the paradox that in the microphysical sphere, the subject (i.e., the observer or his macroscopic prostheses, the measuring instruments), is inevitably part of the process and therefore can never be totally eliminated.

For the classical extroverted thinking type, everything depends on intellectual judgment, and in this he acts according to a formula or a principle derived from the external object. This principle governs all actions and leads the formulation of laws. These laws are declared to be binding for everyone else. Unfortunately this attitude often leads to a certain intellectual tyranny.

Extroverted thinking initially sets out to perceive but also wishes to be applied, which can be embarrassing, especially when it is applied to others, for it can lead to pedantry. This type would do better to stick to things that have a practical application, for as his criterion is taken from outside (extroversion) his actions will always be acceptable. But the extroverted thinker always wants to put his ideal into practice and thus develops a corresponding ethos. Here once again is a risk that the object, whether a thing or a person, will suffer at the expense of the intellectual prerequisites entailed. After all, the objects are measured only by external criteria, such as laws, morals, dogma, principles, and so on. In the sciences, criteria include causality or practicality, which means that theories become one-sided. That is why the extroverted thinking type includes the occasional do-gooder, who fondly imagines that he has reduced all the good or all the evil in the world to a single principle.

The opposite function, in this case, is introverted feeling. The thinking type is often completely unaware of his inferior function, that is, his feeling function. If it ever has an opportunity to express itself, it is expressed in a negative manner. The only time it can be positive is when it is approved by the conscious, which happens only briefly and in small quantities. Feeling's negative "load" manifests itself most frequently in personal susceptibilities and wounded pride. Grudges also fall into this category. Instead of genuine feeling, we have sentimentality and animosity, and the latter can lead to "hysterical" outbursts. In its milder form, the inferior feeling can manifest itself in insights at the level of admitting, "I really should. ..." In the erotic sphere, such people usually tend toward the "participation mystique" and hence toward totally unrealistic, unconscious adulation.

Extroverted thinking + sensation *as an auxiliary function*

Among people who fall into this category we find empirical thinkers, i.e., those whose thinking is based on facts. Under these circumstances, if they have a marked tendency to abstract thinking, they can only be theoreticians. As a result, the terms they coin have a predominantly explanatory character, in contrast, for example, to the classificatory terms of the extroverted sensation types with thinking as an auxiliary function (cf. p. 29). Among these we can include Charles Darwin, for example, but also Ernst Haeckel (1834-1919).

Extroverted thinking + intuition

This combination produces speculative thinking. It would come as no surprise to find such people as Sir James Jeans (1877-1946)[13] or Fred Hoyle (1915) in this category. Generally speaking, it can be said that there is a clear link between mathematical thinking and intuition, which is why we can find many prominent mathematicians in this category.

[13] Cf. James Jeans, *The Universe Around Us*, London 1929.

3. Extroverted feeling

Feeling is a relationship function, in contrast to discriminating thinking. In other words, feeling has a *connecting* function. Feeling types are more likely to be women than men. The feeling is judgmental, although in the case of the extrovert this judgment is geared to objective facts and situations.

Extroverted feeling as the main function

A characteristic of the extroverted feeling type is her perfect adjustment to objective values. If too much importance is attached to the object, it may become difficult to diagnose this type, for this exaggeration can make her quite impersonal and she can even seem cold, for she always makes judgments that are "fitting." On the other hand, the collective, generally accepted values of these people create a very pleasant atmosphere. They are always pleasant, charming and agreeable and thus generate a harmonious social life. They are often active in theater or concert life, in fashion, or in other collective activities, where they are conspicuous for their good taste and friendliness. Generally speaking, their persona is perfect. Adjustment to the external object world can go too far, however, and this then leads to feeling states that are illogical and intermittent. The identity of the ego is lost to the unconscious. In accordance with our 6th fundamental principle (cf. Volume 3, p. 102), the prevailing function in this case is inferior thinking, which leads us on to the subject of the opposite function.

The opposite function in the extroverted feeling type is introverted thinking

In the feeling type, thinking can only follow feeling and is thus dependent and unoriginal. The thinking is usually negativistic and shows signs of primitiveness, such as concretism. Everything is taken at face value, even when intended purely metaphorically. These people are easily influenced because they believe everything they hear. They are often superstitious, and are gullible when it comes to so-called intellectual talk. As they are not capable of independent thinking, their thoughts are subjective and personal, which can make them sound sterile, spiteful and hurtful. William James (1842-1910) criticized this inferior thinking in his *Principles of Psychology* by saying that it always reduces everything to, "It is nothing but ..."[14] This also applies to

Goethe's Mephistopheles, who complements the intuitive feeling type in Faust, who says, "Feeling is all; name is noise and smoke." Another example is a famous researcher, the Dutch physiologist Jacob Mole-schott (1822-1893), who taught at the University of Zurich. For his scientific materialism, man is the sum of his senses. Moleschott wrote the famous aphorisms "no thought without phosphorus" and *Der Mensch ist, was er ißt* [Man is what he eats].

Extroverted feeling + sensation *as an auxiliary function*

People of this type tend to judge everything from an aesthetic point of view. They often have good artistic taste and an excellent sense of style. Their sense of beauty, however, is bound by cultural values and interests them mainly in its historical connection. This is why they are never fashionable, unlike extroverted sensation types with feeling as an auxiliary function (p. 30). If their interests are more practical they often tend to get involved in charity work. Organizers of charitable organizations are usually found in this category, including Henri Dunant (1828-1910), founder of the Red Cross.

Extroverted feeling + intuition

This combination produces men and women who can be described as spiritual mothers. Many priests and doctors fall into this category, but unlike those with sensation combined, their interest is mainly theoretical. This is where we find educators who advocate particular ideals and social innovators.

4. Extroverted intuition

Intuition is a perceiving function and thus, like sensation, is not judging. In extroversion it produces an attitude of expectancy in relation to the external object. The intuition thus creates premonitions about and discoveries of possibilities in the objects, which is why the prevailing attitude is one of expectancy and suggestion. The intuitive is capable of working his way into the object and thus manifesting it. Intuition is never at a loss for a way out of a situation. It constantly seeks to

[14] W. James, *Principles of Psychology*, Harvard 1890.

apprehend new possibilities, which is why it apparently does not allow any real relationship or connection to the object to emerge.

Extroverted intuition as the main function

The extroverted intuitive is attracted to anything embryonic or linked to prospects for the future. He is virtually suffocated by the purely static or by mere being. But, as always, such one-sidedness is partially compensated, in this case by the occasional yearning for something more permanent. This reminds us of Faust's desire to capture the moment because of its beauty. The typical extroverted intuitive abandons anything he has embarked on as soon as possible and despises the secondhand, which he regards as a sort of prison wall. We think here of Adalbert Stifter, who complains about "beginnings without continuations." This is why the intuitive always thinks he has just discovered *the* definitive truth. He has no judgment of his own, which does not interest him because his attitude is purely empirical. This, of course, gives rise to a somewhat questionable morality, based on his loyalty to his own views. But when it happens to him that he does pass judgment, then this judgment, coming from the inferior, unconscious side, has a primitive, infantile or naive character.

This explains why such people show no consideration, either for others or for themselves and their own needs. Even bodily needs are ignored, with the result that such people never relax and constantly overexert themselves. Their lack of attention to the body's needs is commonly shown in the way they either do not eat enough or eat the wrong food. Experience has shown that the stomach usually seeks revenge for this shortcoming, an aspect of what we call psychological localization, as is found, for example, in Yoga (cf. Volume 3, pp. 49-50), and also what A. Adler calls "organ language" (ibid., p. 65). Extroverted intuitives give the impression of being unreliable, because they are always rushing from one thing to another among their many commitments. This rushing around blinds such people to actual reality.

The extroverted intuitive type includes many entrepreneurs, inventors and creators, but also adventurers, globe-trotters, impostors, speculative dealers and swindlers. Intuitive politicians are those who feel that "something has to be done" here today and somewhere else the next day. Not only opportunists but also great discoverers, such as Columbus and Marco Polo, are in this group. On the whole, however, women are usually found in this group, and with their penchant for such things they are in a position to exploit all the social possibilities that arise. If intuition exists to the extent of clairvoyance, such women often use their gifts on a professional basis.

An intuitive, extroverted woman can be not only a source of inspiration but also a destructive vamp. Edouard Schuré has described such cases.[15] It is no secret that Mathilde Wesendonck and Cosima Liszt had this effect on Richard Wagner. A better example is Delphine Potozka with Chopin and a negative one is Georges Sand. It is known that such women often "make" men; but if they become overenthusiastic they are regarded instead as disloyal, for they simply fritter away their lives.

The opposite function in the extroverted intuitive is an introverted sensation. The totally unconscious sensation in this type often leads to compulsive relations to objects or to reality itself, for to some extent such people are "trapped" by the reality. This can even lead to genuine compulsive symptoms. One has the impression that Nature takes revenge on these people for their lack of commitment. Physical ailments flourish, especially those affecting the skin, abdomen, and stomach, a state of affairs described today as psychosomatic. Often, however, compensation is purely psychic, such as phobias, hypochondriac brooding or ridiculous physical sensations. The positive side is that such perceptions may manifest themselves as early warnings of illness, as in the well-known case of Frau Hauffe in Justinus Kerner.[16]

Extroverted intuition + thinking *as the auxiliary function*

This combination tends toward speculation, especially speculative philosophy. Many plans are made and sometimes there can be scientific discoveries. Such types are often in a position to make brilliant business deals, whereas the pure intuitive can never reap the fruits of his perceptions.

Extroverted intuition + feeling

Here we find founders and supporters of idealistic organizations or religious movements (William Booth, founder of the Salvation Army, or Frank Buchman, founder of the so-called Oxford Group Movement).

---

[15] E. Schuré, *Femmes inspiratrices et poètes annonciateurs*, Paris 1907.
[16] J. Kerner, *Die Seherin von Prevorst*, Stuttgart / Tübingen 1829.

B. The Phenomenology of the Functions in Introversion

The introvert's attitude to the object is abstractive. He eliminates the libido from the object as it seems too powerful to him. In fact, he does not really orient himself toward the object at all, but to the "subjective factor." The "numinal accent" therefore rests on the subject. The subjective factor represents a given unconscious disposition, the roots of which go back to the collective unconscious, which makes this disposition "significant" and mythological. Through subjective disposition, the introvert's perceptions and apprehensions are largely adjusted to the subject. In fact he does not perceive the external stimuli as such but rather as their constellation in him as the subject.

In this way the introvert creates for himself a preserve of the ego, and as a result is often criticized for being "subjective," especially by the extrovert. This, however, is a misunderstanding that can give rise to serious conflict. In neutral terms it must be acknowledged that the subject is just as important as the object. It is a prejudice on the part of the extrovert to believe in the automatic superiority of the object. On the other hand, it is perfectly legitimate for the introvert to attach less importance to the pure data of sensation than to his psychological reaction, which merges with the effect produced by the object to create new psychic data. Yet this leads to a devaluation of the object, for the introverted ego attempts to secure itself against the object with every possible and impossible type of freedom, independence, lack of commitment and superiority.

This attitude then leads to a corresponding power complex. But in a compensatory (and inferior) way, thirst for power leads to the need to be loved, which gives the apparently loving object even more power. The result is that one feels the need to "secure" oneself even more firmly against it. This leads to even greater isolation and is the sort of vicious circle studied by A. Adler in particular. With this attitude the relationship to the object is left to the unconscious and thus assumes infantile-primitive-archaic forms, resulting in the object acquiring magical, awe-inspiring qualities.

1. Introverted sensation

For the introverted sensation type the subjective participation of the sensation replaces the external objects (subjective factor). In this way the subject experiences *himself* in the object and his subjective reaction is the most important aspect to him. This explains his inability to give himself to an object; on the contrary, such people retreat from the object. In individual cases it is very difficult to perceive where they retreat to, for what fascinates them are the events and "impressions" of the subjective background, and this is something that third parties do not see. This attitude corresponds to Otto Gross' model of the "prolonged secondary function" (restitution phase). This situation can be understood more vividly if we have the same object painted by different artists, say by an Expressionist, an Impressionist and a Surrealist. The results will show clearly that for these three people the object merely serves as a stimulus for their inner sensations.

Introverted sensation as the main function

If introverted sensation finds expression at all, and this is rarely the case, it will be of an expressionistic nature since the object is replaced by the subjective reaction. But if the means of expression are missing, then the reaction itself remains invisible. As has already been stated, this is often a consequence of the separation of object and subject and the devaluation of the former. If the subjectivity is carried too far, it can lead to an illusory grasp of reality. Such people may regard actual reality as banal and secondary, since they can "see nothing in it or behind it." For this reason, and also because sensation as an irrational function does not pass judgment, such people look inconspicuous, unless they draw attention to themselves by their very inconspicuousness. Usually, however, they seem harmless and the effect they have is to create a rather subdued atmosphere. In the way they behave they are divorced from reality, for as we have already noted, they regard reality as a mere sham.

The opposite function in the introverted sensation type is extroverted intuition. Insofar as the opposite function is repressed, it is predominantly negative. This is why this type notices anything bad or shady and actually senses danger where in fact there is none. The inferior intuition fills him with distrust of his surroundings and produces a negative attitude towards them. In neurotic cases, such fears give rise to symptoms of compulsion and obsessions by forcing the negative intuitions to the surface.

Introverted sensation + thinking *as the auxiliary function*

With the admixture of thinking, such people tend to produce or to believe in categories. However, these principles are acquired on the basis of inadequate empirical material, for their thinking only functions following sensation. For the same reason they are much given to deduction; that is, they are prepared to explain the individual case by deducing from general laws. Although their theories have an anthropomorphic or mythological touch, they often produce unusual and original ideas. A case that springs to mind is Paracelsus. Then there is the amusing example of Friedrich Theodor Vischer (1807-1887), who founded a serious aesthetic movement, only to make fun of it in a novel.[17] In the novel, for example, he allocates the Greek *antas* temple to the "mixture of catarrh and chilblain styles," and the *Peripteros* to the" purely catarrh style." His fascination with the "pitfalls of the object" can also be understood in this way.

Introverted sensation + feeling

Here we find, for example, artists who are extremely problematical, or architects and interior decorators who turn out "living machines" in which it is absolutely impossible to live or chairs on which one cannot sit. One of the artists who managed to give successful expression to this mixture of introverted sensation and feeling was van Gogh, for example. Generally, however, this type expresses itself through somewhat bizarre taste, which purports to be original but is in fact original at all costs. The explanation for this is that the subjective factor is loftily raised to the level of universal validity. Of course such people come across as stubborn and as upholders of unconventional values, and this is in fact a form of clandestine opposition or protest.

2. Introverted thinking

Thinking is a rational function. In the introverted thinker the numinal accent rests on the idea, although this derives not so much from the

[17] F. Th. Vischer, *Auch Einer*, 1879.

object as from the subject. It is thus often based on archetypal concepts, insofar as the idea is understood as the intellectual formulation of these concepts. Jacob Burckhardt's "primordial images" are understood as the preliminary stages of the idea. At this point we should like to quote the passage in Burckhardt's letter of November 11, 1885, to Albert Brenner,[18] where he talks of such "intellectual clarification":

> I have no time for all these special explanations of Faust. And you have surrounded yourself with all sorts of commentaries. Listen: take the whole lot back to the reading rooms where they belong. What you are to find out about Faust will come to you through intuition. For Faust is a genuine myth, i.e. a great primordial image in which each individual has to intuit his being and destiny in his own way. Let me make a comparison: what would the ancient Greeks have said if a commentator had interposed himself between them and the Oedipus legend? In every Greek there was a thread attaching him to the Oedipus legend, and this thread was waiting to be touched and plucked.

And so it is with the German nation and Faust.[19]

Reference must also be made here to Volume 3 (p. 29) of this textbook series where there is a comment on the idea as the content of consciousness, especially as the content of the ego complex and its direct link with the collective unconscious. Because thinking is a rational function, it judges. But the criterion for its judging is given by the subject, so that it is often described as "subjective" in the negative sense of the term. At any rate, it derives from subjectively selected general ideas, and these "obscure" ideas are transformed into "lucid" ones in a way aptly described by Schiller in his letter to Goethe of March 27, 1801. As we have brought in the collective unconscious, let us also quote Goethe's reaction of April 3rd or 4th, 1801, where in our view the phrase "genius of the century" means the constellated contents of the collective unconscious.

Schiller to Goethe 27.3.1801:

[18](1835-1861) a student in Basel at the time. Later a teacher at a Gymnasium in Zürich. Burckhardt was a Professor at the Federal Institute of Technology in Zürich.
[19]Cf. Jacob Burckhardt's *Briefe* (Critical edition by Max Burckhardt, Basel 1955, Vol. III, p. 228).

Just a few days ago I declared war on Schelling because of a claim he made in his transcendental philosophy that "in Nature one starts from the unconscious in order to raise it to consciousness, whereas in Art one proceeds from the conscious to the unconscious." Granted, he is only dealing here with the contrast between the product of Nature and the product of Art, and he is quite right as far as that goes. I fear, however, that these gentlemen idealists, because of their ideas, pay scant attention to experience, and it is in experience that the poet, too, starts off just from the conscious; indeed, he must consider himself fortunate if, through the clearest awareness of his processes, he manages just to get to the stage of recognizing the original dark total idea of his work in undiluted from in the final product. Without such a dark, but powerful total idea, which precedes all the technical aspects, there can be no poetic work, and the essence of poetry, it seems to me, lies in this very ability to express the unconscious and convey it to others, i.e., transfer it onto an object.

Goethe's reply:

Referring to the questions in your last letter, I not only share your opinion but would even go further. I believe that anything that genius does as genius comes about unconsciously. The man of genius can use his common sense and behave in accordance with his convictions after giving the matter due consideration, but these are not his priorities. No work of genius can be improved by reflection and its immediate consequences, or have its errors eliminated; but through reflection and action genius can attain the stage where it ultimately brings forth exemplary works. The more geniuses the century has, the more the individual is advanced.[20]

The introverted thinker goes in for new views rather than new facts, the latter being used at best as illustrations. His conclusions are oriented to the subject, in fact come from and lead to the subject, whereas extroverted thinking leads from the object to the object. In view of the introvert's inadequate link to the object, he does not express himself, which makes it difficult to describe this type. He is strong on the *essence* of something and weak on words. A good illustration of this is the following tale, which should perhaps be taken with a pinch of scepticism.

A Christian is continually thrown into the arena but the wild beasts never touch him. Caesar finally summons him and promises him his freedom in return for revealing his secret. The would-be martyr says that he lets the lion

[20] trans. D.R.

get close and then whispers in his ear: "Would you please say a few words after the meal."

The apparently extremely introverted lion loses his appetite at the thought of having to make an after-dinner speech.

Introverted thinking as the main function

It is safe to say that the life of the introverted thinking type is governed by the idea and, as we have already stated, this idea derives from the subjective factor. In contrast to the extrovert, however, this idea is not put into practice; nor is it applied to others or even recommended to them. In this respect it is just wishful thinking, or, at worst, resentment. This type has no faith in society and is thus easily discouraged. When he starts to form an idea he does so just for its own sake and then tends to idealize it and subordinate everything to it. On the other hand, he makes no attempt to put this ideal into practice, or if he does, then only in relation to himself. Thus the introverted thinking type remains alienated from the world. He often tends to be self-destructive in his severe self-criticism. And yet, as he remains with the subject, he will never turn into a do-gooder, although, he secretly longs to be one. This often gives his thinking an original or even whimsical note.

A classical example of this type is I. Kant, whose introversion manifested itself in the fact that he never felt the need to leave Koenigsberg. A. Schopenhauer also falls into this category, and this emerged particularly in his oddness. The following quotations will show that this is also the case with the transcendental idealist R.W. Emerson (Boston 1803-1882):

The eye is the first circle; the horizon which it forms is the second; and throughout nature this primary figure is repeated without end. It is the highest emblem in the cipher of the world. St. Augustine described the nature of God as a circle whose center was everywhere, and its circumference nowhere. We are all our lifetime reading the copious sense of this first of forms. One moral we have already deduced in considering the circular or compensatory character of every human action. Another analogy we shall now trace – that every action admits of being outdone. Our life is an apprenticeship to the truth, that around every circle another can be drawn; that there is no end in nature, but every end is a beginning; that there is always another dawn risen on mid-noon, and under every deep a lower deep opens.

The key to everyman is his thought. Sturdy and defying though he look, he has a helm which he obeys, which is the idea after which all his facts ar classified. He can only be reformed by showing him a new idea which commands his own. The life of a man is a self-evolving circle, which, from a ring imperceptibly small, rushes on all sides outwards to new and larger circles, and that without end. The extent to which this generation of circles, wheel without wheel, will go, depends on the force or truth of the individual soul. For it is the inert effort of each thought, having formed itself into a circular way of circumstance – as, for instance, an empire, rules of an art, a local usage, a religious rite – to heap itself on that ridge, and to solidify, and hem in the life. But if the soul is quick and strong, it bursts over that boundary on all sides, and expands another orbit on the great deep, which also runs up into a high wave, with attempts again to stop and to bind. But the heart refuses to be imprisoned; in its first and narrowest pulse it already tends outward with a vast force, and to immense and innumerable expansions....

Beware when the great God lets loose a thinker on this planet. Then all things are at risk. It is as when a conflagration has broken out in a great city, and no man knows what is safe, or where it will end. There is not a piece of science, but its flank may be turned tomorrow; there is not any literary reputation, not the so-called eternal names of fame, and may not be revised and condemned. The very hopes of man, the thoughts of his heart, the religion of nations, the manners and morals of mankind, are all at the mercy of a new generalization. Generalization is always a new influx of the divinity into the mind. Hence the thrill that attends it.[21]

It is highly probable that certain alchemists, such as Gerardus Dorneus or Michael Maier, were introverted thinkers.

The opposite function of the introverted thinking type is extroverted feeling. As an inferior function it has a negative effect, for example in the form of susceptibilities. It can manifest itself in primitive outbursts or in incredibly fantastic emotional relationships or judgments. When feeling breaks through in an introverted thinking type, he can be kind to a fault. What then happens to him is that he overrates inferior objects out of all proportion. He is also afraid of the unknown, in the case of a man, often afraid of women. As it grows, this misogyny can turn into misanthropy in general and may alienate him from the world. As such people have no empathy, they make poor teachers. This reminds us of Ostwald's description of *Helmholtz* (pp. 89-91 in Volume 3). Yet

[21] R.W. Emerson, *Essays* III, Halle n.d.

people who belong to this group have a great capacity for enthusiasm on the one hand, and on the other are easily offended and thus driven into loneliness. Their occasional gullibility and suggestibility through personal influence is amazing, made possible by the fact that the path goes through the unconscious (extroverted feeling). Many of these people fight an ongoing battle in the resistance to extroverted feeling and this can lead to chronic exhaustion, formerly referred to as neurasthenia or psychasthenia.

Introverted thinking + sensation *the auxiliary functions*

This combination produces empirical thinking, with the main consideration given to those facts that coincide with the preexisting idea. Empirical material is accumulated by such people until the idea seems secured. They brood over their ideas for a very long time and are slow to publicize them. An idea may be explained, but not the road that led to it. In fact, the tracks that led to the idea are wiped out, although one must admit the difficulty of showing clearly how one came by an idea. We refer here to the comments made by Ostwald about the mathematician Gauss, as quoted on p. 91 of Volume 3. Here the idea is explained, but not the path that led to it and in doing this the author demands too much of the listener or the reader, for his language is too abstract and too concentrated. The reason is that for this type the images in their inner vividness are clear; the idea explains itself to him, with the result that he never asks himself how he came to it.

Introverted thinking + intuition

The intuitive components of this combination lead to direct perception of the subjective factor and so this type soon lapses into a world of unreality. For him the psychic phenomenon takes on aspects of reality; his statements automatically contain elements of the unconscious. Here we meet philosophers with a speculative tendency and with premonitions about the future. They are usually not understood in the present, Schopenhauer being a case in point. Another telling example is Nietzsche. Others with this combination of introverted thinking and intuition are philosophers of the occult, although one hardly dare mention them by name.

3. Introverted feeling

As a rational function, feeling makes deductions, judges and evaluates. With introversion, however, this evaluation orients itself totally according to the criterion of the subjective factor. This creates the appearance that real objects are devalued, which is why this type gives the impression of being cool and indifferent. This sometimes makes diagnosis difficult, for feeling types are naively expected to give an impression of warmth. Let us not forget, however, that this apparent coldness represents a defense mechanism on the part of the introvert because he feels overwhelmed by the external objects, and when feeling has no outlet it is difficult to perceive.

Introverted feeling as the main function

This type is principally found among women. It is not easy to describe and is often misunderstood. This type makes no attempt to show regard for others, for they are really aware only of themselves. Such people are inclined to melancholy and a harmonious adjustment to the object situation, but only so long as none of their feeling values is offended. For the same reason they are benevolent but neutral in the face of any show of enthusiasm. They are the proverbial "still waters that run deep," disapproving of any form of passion. Only in the projection onto children do they find it easy to show their feelings. The values that are so cherished by this type are not collective but are highly individual, if not mystical and ecstatic, which is particularly fascinating for the extroverted man. Their feelings are not extensive but intensive. They are kind and friendly in a secret sort of way and so are never conspicuous. In this category we find secret benefactors who make personal sacrifices, rather than philanthropists. Their commonest role is that of the quiet companion who is totally dependable. They never draw attention to themselves but are firm and incorruptible to the point of stubbornness, and their morality is often surprisingly unconventional.

A good representative of the introverted type is, in our view, Francesco Patrizzi, also known as Franciscus Patritius or Patricius (1529-1597).[22] He taught philosophy at the University of Ferrara from 1578 to 1592, and then in Rome until his death. His writings show him

[22] Cf. P.O. Kristeller, *Eight Philosophers of the Italian Renaissance*, Stanford Calif. 1964, Chap. VII.

to be one of the best-read men of his age. Judging from his most important work, *Nova de universis philosophia* (Venetiis 1591), it is possible to describe his orientation as pantheistic naturalism; the deified cosmos has a unified life for him, which is a return to the tenet of the anima mundi. Ever since Albertus Magnus and Thomas Aquinas, official Church teachings had been dominated by Aristotelianism, but Patrizzi, running counter to current fashion, came out in favor of Platonism. In the foreword of his main work he urgently pleads with his former schoolfriend, Pope Gregory XIV, to exert all his influence to ensure that the Church eliminates the ungodly Aristotle and replaces him with Patrizzi's pious Platonic teachings.

The opposite function of the introverted feeling type is extroverted thinking. This inferior thinking is correspondingly primitive and con-cretistic, leading to bibliolatry or slavish adherence to facts. In its negative mode it inclines to destructive and venomous criticism, espe-cially of other people, but also of the world in general. Such people always know "what others are thinking," including nasty remarks (projection), and the consequence is that they themselves get involved in compensatory intrigues. Generally speaking, they are inclined to be pessimistic, to make personal misinterpretations and deprecating "ex-planations." Such people thus succumb to the power of the object and seek the error in the conclusion instead of the premise.

Introverted feeling + sensation *as the auxiliary function*

This mixture produces an "aesthetic" orientation with a highly individual and original taste, which is completely independent. In artists this gives rise to a mild form of expressionism with a touch of human-ism, as in Paul Klee, for example. Many religious people fall into this category, especially priests, monks and nuns, and doctors. People of this type can really be models. In our opinion the general tone of this mixture is best epitomized by Buddhism, in which *pity* for suffering is a factor, and in Zen, in which there is a strong emphasis on sensation and meditation.

Introverted feeling + intuition

These people have a tendency toward self-development according to the criteria of their inner experience. Here, too, we come across reli-gious people, who feel the need to put their inner experiences into practice in their personal lives. This is why many mystics are found here. The general tone of early Christianity, with its emphasis on *agape* is undoubtedly rooted in this type. Among the poets it is the lyric poets who are most strongly represented. One who springs to mind is Robert Browning (1812-1889), with his love of mankind, and another is Hölderlin, at least as long as he remained in good health.

4. Introverted intuition

As an irrational perception function, intuition in introversion is oriented toward the perception of possibilities (especially as regards the future), derived from the material of the unconscious, insofar as it lies behind actual reality. In this way the separation of events in space or time is skipped over in favor of coincidences on the level of the collective unconscious (synchronistic connections).

Introverted intuition is really a paradoxical function. Because it is oriented toward inner material, its objects are largely contents of the unconscious. In other words, it is only psychic reality that counts. And yet, as we stated in the epistemological section of Volume 3 of this textbook series, this reality is not actually accessible to any experience. (Let us not forget that in principle this also applies to external objects insofar as what we perceive can be only an initial approach.) But in introverted intuition the subjective factor becomes a relevant force, for subjective contents are viewed subjectively, and the subjectivity thus increases. Introverted intuition thus perceives simultaneous background processes of the conscious, and these unconscious images actually become things or objects. It is characteristic of the introverted intuitive that he does not make the connection between these perceptions and himself (his ego). In other words, for him the perception is simply an "aesthetic phenomenon," nothing more than an unreflected perception, a "sensation." Thus it can never become a moral problem. The extrovert, when he meets such a person, condemns him as someone who "clings to pointless dreams" and is not in touch with reality.

What is really perceived through introverted intuition are the archetypal images or sequence patterns of the circumstances of human life. And as the introverted intuitive perceives such sequence patterns, he is also in a position to predict how they will continue.

Introverted intuition as the main function

Prophets, visionaries and psychics are common among people of this types. They live in the rarified atmosphere of visions of the future, and in so doing are perfectly capable of ruthlessly trampling over reality and tradition. This is why they are often revolutionaries, innovators and leaders. In his book *Neue Menschen,* Knud Rasmussen gives an account of a classical leader figure among the Polar Eskimos.[23] He spent a year among these people at the North Pole and he learned that many years earlier their hunting grounds had become exhausted and the people were faced with starvation. Then a man, we would call him a shaman, promised his people new hunting grounds in the west. As they followed him, they travelled westward for two and a half years and reached Baffin Bay; in other words they had crossed Greenland to America, and that is how they were saved. Some of the tribe had turned back half way through, having lost faith in their leader, and they came to a sad end. Another leader, Adolf Hitler, led his people to their downfall because he was overwhelmed by the breakthrough of extroverted sensation as inferior function. It seems to depend on the stars as to whether such dreamers are simply misunderstood or whether they are actually hopeless builders of castles in the air. At any rate we find here many "unappreciated geniuses" and "voices in the wilderness," such as Emanuel Swedenborg (1688-1772) or William Blake (1757-1827). Edouard Schuré, Wagner's promoter in France, dedicated his work, *Les grands initiés*[24] to such personalities, and his own fantasies are documented in the book *La pretresse d'Isis.* Pierre Benoit's (1886-1962) *L'Atlantide,*[25] or Rider Haggard's (1856-1925) amazing analogue *She* (1887),[26] may be described as classical representations of such images from the depths.

It is not easy to convey to the reader what the psychologist sees in this type of literature. We are arrogant enough to declare that what these authors are doing is expressing their unconscious processes. The end product can be a success or a failure. It can be rubbish or a great work of art. Among the successes we can certainly count Goethe's *Faust II,* or the "fairy tale" in the *Unterhaltungen deutscher Ausgewanderter.*

[23] Knud Rasmussen, *Neue Menschen*, Bern 1907, p. 26ff.
[24] Ed. Schuré, *Les grands initiés*, Paris 1889.
[25] P. Benoit, *L'Atlantide*, Paris 1919.
[26] H. Rider Haggard, *She*, London 1887.

Others are Spitteler's *Prometheus* and the *Olympian Spring,* as well as E.T.A. Hoffmann's *Elixiere des Teufels,* or *Der goldne Topf*[27]. Just to show how much material the unconscious provides for literary purposes, we shall now give a list of works that have a flavor of the unconscious: all the novels by Gustav Meyrink, *Das Reich ohne Raum* (ca. 1920) by Bruno Goetz, Oskar Panizza's *Visionen der Dämmerung* (1922) and especially the fantastic novel by the painter and sculptor Alfred Kubin, *Die andere Seite* (1923). But to give this genre of literature its full due, we should like to refer to its ancient predecessors, such as the Baruch and Henoch apocrypha in the Old Testament and to John's apocalypse in the New Testament. The whole *Corpus Hermeticum* is of great significance in the psychology of religion, especially the "Poimandres" with its heathen gnosis.[28] The same spirit permeates the recently discovered Coptic-gnostic texts of Nag-Hammadi, such as the "Evangelium Veritatis" *(Codex Jung)*[29]. What is more, early Greek alchemy abounds in such texts, one example being the treatise of Komarios[30] from the 1st century.[31]

Extroverted sensation as the opposite function of introverted intuition

As an inferior function, sensation is archaic and instinctual. It tends toward excessiveness, being invoked exclusively with sensual impressions, which can lead to compulsive ties and sensations. The introverted intuitive, as a result of his inferior extroverted sensation, has a negative relationship to reality, and hence often makes himself extremely unpopular. The reverse side of this is that he himself hates given facts, or at least holds them in contempt. This can manifest itself in the "constructing" of special enemies, such as the Freemasons, the Jews, the Jesuits or the Blacks. But reality gains its revenge for such unjust attitudes by

[27] Cf. A. Jaffé, *Bilder und Symbole aus E.T.A. Hoffmanns "Der goldne Topf",* Daimon, Einsiedeln, 1990.
[28] Corpus Hermeticum, ed. A.D. Nock and A.-J. Festugière, Paris 1960, 5 vols.
[29] Evangelium Veritatis, in: *Codex Jung,* ed. M. Malinine, H.-Ch. Puech, G. Quispel, Zürich 1956.
[30] Book by Komarios, the philosopher and high priest, who taught Cleopatra the divine and sacred art of the philosophers' stone. Repr. Holland Press, London 1963, V, p. 278 ff.
[31] M.P.E. Berthelot (1827-1907), *Collection des anciens alchimistes grecs,* Paris 1888.

placing pitfalls in the way of these people, in the form, for example, of compulsive ties to unsuitable people or things.

Introverted intuition + thinking *as the auxiliary function*

This combination produces intuitive philosophers, for example, whose thinking relies on intuition. Such people as Boehme or Gichtel belong here, and also C.G. Garus and many of the Romantics. A particularly good example is the younger Fichte (1797-1879), Immanuel Hermann Fichte, the son of Johann Gottlieb Fichte, who advocated ethical theism. For him the soul is a "spirit monad" with a pre-empirical character (we would say archetypes). He regards consciousness as an attendant symptom of the spiritual processes, which in themselves are unconscious. God is compared to creative thinking, which preceded and still precedes the world.[32] This combination has also produced several of the hermetic philosophers as well as many inventors.

Introverted intuition + feeling

Here we frequently find religious people who are particularly fond of belonging to small groups of new religious movements. In our view, *Hölderlin,* at the time that he was mentally ill, moved into this state. Previously he had tended more toward a certain aestheticism; i.e., extroverted sensation predominated. The pathological breakthrough was achieved through introverted intuition, originally an inferior function.

Categories of this nature are, of course, always problematical and must be understood only as references. If we conclude with the conjecture that atonal music and certain recent musical developments originate with people with this combination, then we do so with great reservations.

[32] Cf. R. Mehlich, *I.H. Fichtes Seelenlehre*, Zürich 1935.

Chapter III

The Compass

Now that we have described the four extroverted and the four introverted types as briefly as possible, it should have become clear that the Jungian tenet of psychological types, which is based on two opposite attitudes and two pairs of opposite functions, can be traced back to the ancient idea of opposite principles. Generally speaking, people tend to remain unconscious of their own contradictions for as long as possible, and in this they are aided and abetted by modern civilization, which places all sorts of facilities at their disposal, legitimate or otherwise, all of which are appreciated and approved by the public at large. Thus, in Jung's terms, the opposite function can remain largely unconscious for a long time. This means that it cannot stand in opposition to consciousness and that consequently no moral problem arises. Of course the opposite function is still there but reveals itself only indirectly; for opposites exist only in consciousness, i.e., only when both components of consciousness are represented. Jung used to illustrate this with the example of muscle innervation: if we make a specific voluntary movement, we are only aware of the synergetic innervation, but we are not aware of the antagonistic innervation, which is simultaneous and important for the control of the movement.

Inner contradiction normally manifests itself in our dreams, which we discussed in Volume 2 of this textbook series. Unfortunately, and sometimes to our detriment, it can also make its presence felt in the form of unwelcome disturbances of our conscious process.

The attitude type (extroversion or introversion) seems to be genetically given, but this seems to be less the case with the selection of the main function, in which the influences of one's surroundings seem more important. A major role is played by family tradition and the spirit of the times. Later the "selection" is reinforced by the factors entailed in the choice of profession. The function that is already the preferred one is then trained to adapt to the principle of achievement, whether one likes it or not. Although the numinal accent is already present, this process reinforces it; the fascination of the differentiated function is increased, so that its differentiation is automatically continued as in a feedback system.

The one-sided emphasis of the differentiated function is, as we have stated, indispensable, but it can lead to a distortion of the whole personality. The classical *déformation professionnelle* is an example of this. Goethe described this terrible dilemma accurately in his "note" on "Ernst Stiedenroth, *Psychologie zur Erklärung der Seelenerscheinungen* 1. Teil, Berlin 1834":

> On many an occasion I have expressed the displeasure I felt as a young man at the tenet of inferior and superior spiritual forces. In the human spirit, as in the universe, there is neither below nor above – everything is equally entitled to a common middle point, which manifests its secret being through the harmonious relationship of all parts. All disputes, be they ancient or modern, stem from the splitting up of what God in his nature brought forth as an entity. We know full well that in individual human natures there is usually a preponderance of some feature or ability and that this necessarily leads to a one-sided approach to matters, in that man only knows the world through himself and thus naively and presumptuously believes that the world has been built up by him and for his sake. This is why he places his main talents in the foreground, and anything inferior about himself he categorically disclaims and even tries to eradicate from his totality. Anyone who is not convinced that he has to weld into a whole all the manifestations of human nature – sensuality and reason, fantasy and common sense – whichever one predominates in him, will be reduced to an unpleasantly limited existence, never understanding why he has so many obdurate opponents and why he sometimes even places himself in the role of the outsider. Thus a man born and bred in the so-called exact sciences, at the very peak of his powers of reasoning, will not find it easy to understand that there can also be an exact sensual fantasy, without which there can actually be no art. There is the same point of contention between the disciples of a religion of feeling and one of reason; unless the latter are willing to concede that religion starts with feeling, the former will refuse to admit that they should strive for common sense."[33]

In Vol. 3 of this textbook series (p. 82-7), we attempted to show how this problem of opposites became a problem for Schiller. It was also made clear that any one-sidedness, i.e., unconsciousness, is immoral.

[33] Goethe, *Nachgelassene Werke*. Zur Naturwissenschaft im Allgemeinen.

It is, however, only in rare cases that one-sidedness is as bad as all that, for what usually happens is that alongside the main function there is at least one other relatively well-differentiated one. Of course, all the products of the various functions can be conscious, but we say that the function is differentiated only when its practice is decisive in the orientation of consciousness and is totally available to the exercise of will at all times. For example, if I, with my thinking, am able to understand the intellectual observations of another thinker, this does not mean that my thinking may be regarded as differentiated. That is only true when I am in a position to solve thinking problems on my own, without any great effort on my part.; for the main function acts as a matter of course and is thus decisive for the type concerned because it is totally reliable and claims absolute validity, unlike the animals in the witches' kitchen (Goethe, *Faust I*).

> If we can but succeed
> And things fit indeed,
> Then thoughts we show...

As soon as the activating of a function involves effort, rather than happening as a matter of course, then one or another of the auxiliary functions is usually involved. As a merely auxiliary function, however, it must not stand in opposition to the main function (exclusion principle, 3rd fundamental principle). If opposition exists, the diagnosis would need to be reassessed. In this connection, it must be noted that there cannot be any crass opposition between the two possible auxiliary functions, for they are both relatively unconscious.

It must be recalled at this point that in a primitive state of mind such problems of opposites just do not arise, for all the functions are relatively equally conscious or unconscious – in fact they are in a sort of primordial harmony. Thus for these people there is one functioning, which is often felt as soothingly holistic and even, from a romantic point of view, as pleasant. J.G. Seume's expression, *"Wir Wilden sind doch bessere Menschen"* ("we wild ones are better people" J.G. Seume) explains Rousseau's desire to "return to Nature." But the gods have made us conscious and "guilty," depriving us of the possibility of annulling the Fall of Man. Our only alternative, if we are to achieve wholeness again, is the painstaking path of cultural effort, in psychological terms the acquisition of consciousness, and in Jungian terms the path to individuation. In our view, a particularly impressive attempt to do this is H. v. Kleist's essay, "Über das Marionettentheater" (1810).

All further observations in this volume are based on the following two premises:

1. It is true that the inferior function is in opposition to the main function, in the way that we stated in our formulation of the exclusion principle (3rd fundamental principle). However, because it is essentially similar to the main function, according to the 2nd fundamental principle, then it can successfully emerge as a *competitive* function. Let us take a thinking type (main function = thinking); his inferior feeling will also come over as a *rational* function, just like his thinking. In the same way, sensation and intuition, both irrational functions, are also essentially alike; but this fact in no way reduces the element of opposition between the main function and the inferior one.
2. The auxiliary functions, on the other hand, especially the first one, can actually *serve* the main function, because they do not directly oppose or compete with it.

To make the following observations more clear, let us refer to the diagram in Figure 5, below. First, however, a few preliminary remarks are called for: the four consciousness functions make up a quaternio. Its origins, according to Jung's thinking, are completely irrational. Jung first came across this image in his "occult" work with his cousin Helly Preiswerk.[34] After that he was always under its spell, so much so that it can safely be said that the rest of his life's work was given over to the amplification and deeper substantiation of his quaternity image. The chronology of this development has been dealt with elsewhere.[35] For Jung the four functions have to be multiplied by two, for they also come under either the extroverted or the introverted attitude. With his book, Psychological Types (1921), and to the end of his life, his vast clinical experience showed him that with the development of the personality, i.e., with individuation, there must be an attempt to make all four functions conscious in the course of time – in other words, to differen-

---

[34]C.G. Jung, On the Psychology and Pathology of so-called Occult Phenomena, CW 1, pars. 63ff. German original 1902.
[35]C.A. Meier, *Experiment und Symbol*, Olten 1975, pp. 193-211.

tiate them as much as possible. So his "compass" proved itself in more than one way. A forerunner of Jung's "compass" was an aphorism of Georg Christoph Lichtenberg (1742-1799):[36] "The reasons that motivate us to do something could be classified like the thirty-two winds, with their names being formed in the same way, e.g., bread-bread-fame or fame-fame-bread."

The question now is whether it is possible to deduce laws or even predict them from the quaternity schema for this process of becoming conscious (cf. Figure 5).

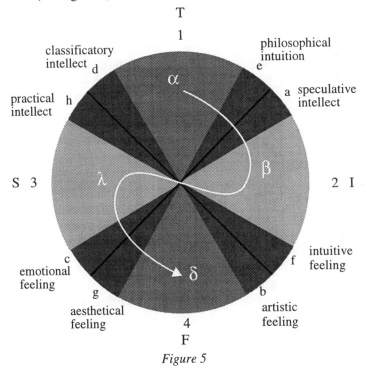

Figure 5

In Figure 5 let us assume, for the sake of argument, that we are dealing with a thinking type (1) with intuition (2) as the first auxiliary function (quadrant 1 and parts of quadrant 2). Should the need or necessity arise for him to extend the basis of his consciousness, then at first he will concentrate on that tendency which is already present,

[36] Georg Christoph Lichtenberg, *Vermischte Schriften*, Vol. II, Göttingen 1844, p. 54.

namely intuitive thinking (1 a), and this will lead him to develop a speculative intellect (intuition as a function of thinking). Once this combination is functioning satisfactorily, and intuition is being given its full due and is largely at the disposal of consciousness, then there arises the question of how the process can continue. As thinking will continue to cling to its dominant position, the transition from here (intuition) to feeling (4) as the inferior function is still "forbidden," because of the exclusion principle (3rd fundamental principle). However, sensation (3) does not stand in such sharp contrast to intuition, since the latter, being merely an auxiliary function, does not have as strong a potential as does thinking. This being the case, thinking offers itself as the next step in the transition toward 3 (5). Once sensation has been given more consideration and has thus experienced a certain differentiation, it can be used as a second auxiliary function. As the final step towards becoming whole, feeling (4) has to be integrated into the consciousness system. This turns out to be a rather difficult matter. Although it is true that in this transition there is no direct tension of opposites, thinking still regards feeling negatively. While sensation is largely unconscious, feeling languishes away in almost total obscurity, and like all unconscious contents, it can be made accessible only indirectly.

We shall have to leave it at that for the moment; later we shall go into the clinical aspects of individuation. Just a word here about the choice of colors allocated to the various functions: blue, for thinking, corresponds to the coolness of the thinking world; red, for feeling, is the color of warmth, like our blood; green, for sensation, is the predominant color in our world, and thus stands for the *fonction du réel*. Yellow, for intuition, is rather awkward, like the function itself. When our analysands pick up pencils or crayons to express their experiences, it turns out that our color classification is virtually a standard one; this, however, needs to be confirmed statistically by larger numbers. Jung also managed to support his arguments with ethnological material from all over the world, thus giving them an amazingly objective universality.

By way of further remarks on Figure 5, let us add that in addition to colors, we have also given the functions numbers. The numbers 1-4 are intended to show the order in which the differentiation of the functions will occur in the course of the individuation process in the example of a thinking type. In our example we have taken a thinking type (1) whose first auxiliary function is intuition (2). This admixture (a) gives his intellect a speculative touch. With someone who has intuition (2) as the main function and thinking as the first auxiliary function, the effect of the combination would be that with the help of his thinking he would transfer his intuitive vision into the sphere of understanding, thus acquiring a philosophical intuition (1e). However, if his first auxiliary function is feeling (4), this overlapping (4b) will produce an artistic intuition, one which selects its images with feeling (cf. Chap. II for the extroverted type and the introverted type in each combination).

In someone with sensation as the main function (3), the predominance of thinking as the first auxiliary function produces a classificatory intellect; on the other hand, the overlapping with feeling as the first auxiliary function (3c) would result in emotional feelings. With the feeling type (4), there is the possibility that he might have intuition as the first auxiliary function (overlapping 2f), which would result in intuitive feeling. An alternative possibility is that sensation is the first auxiliary function, which then produces a feeling colored by aesthetic factors (4g) (cf. chap. II for the extroverted type and the introverted type in each of the above combination).

It should be pointed out here that, for example, in the first case (main function = feeling, 1st auxiliary function = intuition), in accordance with the exclusion principle (3rd fundamental principle), feeling is more strongly inhibited than intuition, insofar as this combination functions as the unconscious opposite type to practical intellect (3h). This rule applies to all the other possible combinations, with the appropriate changes being made, of course. In Figure 5 we have drawn an S-shaped line that is intended to show the temporal sequence of the differentiation of functions in the individuation process. It must be kept in mind that the strict exclusion principle is modified as soon as we are no longer dealing with the sharp contrast between main function and inferior function, but rather with the weaker contrast between two relatively unconscious auxiliary functions; for opposites only exist where there is consciousness.

Chapter IV

Theoretical Conclusions

As mentioned in Chapter III, Jung discovered the quaternio very early in his dealings with the human psyche. A little later, on the basis of the results of the Association Experiment (cf. Vol. 1 of this textbook series), he ascertained the duality of the attitude types (introverted and extroverted). He tried to use the concept of duality to reconcile the attitude typologies of Freud and Adler, but his efforts were to no avail. Freud did not become an Adlerian, nor Adler a Freudian, and neither of them became a Jungian. These differences of opinion have raged undiminished for decades up to the present day. Evidence of this conflict, unfortunately, is the almost desperate tenacity with which they cling to attitude and function. And the differences will remain, even when the domestic troubles of the psychological schools have long been a thing of the past. Schools of any kind are simply unwilling to accept that they can be taught anything; and once we belong to a school, we do not learn anything new, for within the group we are sheltered from doubt by the collective.

In contrast to this, Jung could be compared to Terence: *homo sum, nil humani a me alienum puto* (I am a human being, nothing human is alien to me). In practice his typological quaternio proved to be an archetype, a given factor in our psyche. It is a feature of archetypes that in some inexplicable way they will manifest, if not actually assert, themselves in the course of our lives. And when, as with the psychological quaternio, an archetype is a fundamental structure of our psyche, then it will demand its due, regardless of circumstances, even if it should take a lifetime, which is often the case. The typological schema served Jung as a pattern for this process (cf. the S-shaped line in Figure 5, p. 57), and the process itself could be observed in countless cases during analytical work. As is so often the case with findings in depth psychology, this clinically proven fact is the outcome of work with ill people, for the path is difficult and rarely undertaken on a voluntary basis. Granted, we have heard Schiller's cry (Vol. 3 of this textbook series, p. 82), but he was fully aware of the awesome task involved:

> In that nether world of terror,
> And man shall not tempt the gods.
> Let him never yearn to see
> What they veil with night and horror!
>
> *– The Diver*

A similar warning is sounded by his opposite type, Goethe:

> Two souls alas, are housed within my breast,
> And each will wrestle for the mastery there.
> The one has passion's craving for crude love,
> And hugs a world where sweet the senses rage;
> The other longs for pastures fair above,
> Leaving the murk for lofty heritage."
>
> *– Faust I,* "Outside the Town gate"

A further example for the two souls is found in Victor Hugo:

> Si j'écoute mon coeur, j'entends un dialogue;
> Nous sommes deux au fond de mon esprit.
> (If I listen to my heart, I hear a dialogue;
> In the depths of my spirit we are two.)
>
> *– "L'année terrible,"* 1872

Let us try to understand the justification for these warnings. It is based on the fact that in the so-called normal healthy organism, consciousness is compensated by the unconscious. All this means is that normally a state of equilibrium exists between the two systems, one of which is metastable.[37] In other words, the contrast can normally remain unconscious without being missed in the whole system, although closer observation of the consciousness of such a person will reveal one-sidedness. On the whole, however, this one-sidedness does not disturb us, or only on certain occasions.

We have already discussed the sudden change that usually occurs in the course of life, at the so-called turn of life. From the aspect of typology, it represents a breakthrough of the previously unconscious functions and thus the opposite attitude. The "slips" we referred to in

---

[37] The expression derives from W. Ostwald and serves to describe the phase of an oversaturated solution.

Volume I of this textbook series can be seen as microphenomena, or as harbingers of this change. They usually last for a short time, however, and are rarely so dramatic or traumatic that we feel we must make sweeping changes in our attitudes. On the whole they are merely unpleasant and are thus repressed as quickly as possible.

In the individual cases of the various main functions above, the effects of the relevant inferior functions also fall into the category of temporary disturbances. They most commonly manifest themselves in states of fatigue or toxic conditions and may also involve defense mechanisms (repressions). But as the turn of life approaches, these defense mechanisms become less and less effective. From the viewpoint of Jungian typology this is a failure of the domination of the archetype in favor of wholeness – the quaternio – which gradually begins to assert itself, sometimes even against our will. The change that then occurs is a permanent one.

Three different causes of this kind of change can be clinically ascertained:

1. When the one-sided emphasis and exclusive preference for the differentiated function in life has gone on too long. In such cases the breakthrough can have a liberating effect.
2. When a massive breakthrough of unconscious contents occurs spontaneously, which can be seen as a "creative" experience.
3. When the breakthrough is brought about through a traumatic disturbance of the differentiated function as a result of external influences.

Let us take a closer look at this breakthrough phenomenon. The emphasizing of the differentiated function is, as we have said, a vital necessity (déformation professionnelle). It is in the essence of consciousness that the field of vision is completely dominated by the respective content. But what is important today can become unimportant tomorrow. Consciousness exaggerates everything it is currently dealing with; but because of its need for continuity, it brings to light things that would otherwise be regarded as irrelevant or would be completely ignored. Primitive consciousness is known to be very imprecise. This explains, for example, why all vultures were female for the ancient Egyptians, why mares were impregnated by the wind for the Greeks, and why the ancient Chinese believed that all turtles were female and were impregnated by male serpents. There are similar examples in psychology, at least up to the 17th century, when it was believed, for example, that gold shone in the dark. Today, by way of contrast, we "suffer" from a consciousness that has become very precise, having specialized in *one* function, the so-called main function. It takes its objects very seriously and does not shrink from any unpleasantness or small matter, however trivial it may seem. Nothing is insignificant, except what one overlooks or represses. This means that consciousness and the differentiated function is greatly extended, but only in one direction; in other words, it becomes exclusive and represses the opposite (inferior) function all the more. The subject flows away into the infinite, if not into a void. This is where the danger lies in specialization, which can lead to dilettantism in all other spheres (e.g., in psychology). It should be recalled, by the way, that the literal meaning of *dilettare* (Lat. *delecto*) is "to take delight in," and *dilettarsi dun arte* actually means to pursue an art form seriously.

Let us remind ourselves once again of how the suppressed reverse side expresses itself in the four function types:

- The S type does not see any world of possibilities; the feelings about the future are apprehensive and filled with unpleasant suspicions (inferior, negative intuition).
- The T type has a childish and archaic feeling world, at best – for example, a sentimental sense of family or fanciful feelings (inferior feeling).
- The F type exhibits a primitive, childish thinking, confused when it comes to personalism, and is thus traditionalistic and possibly paranoid (inferior thinking).
- The I type views reality as a dangerous trap (inferior sensation).

In contrast to the above, it must be stated that the world can have meaning only when man as an entity can experience it as an entity. To do that he must be whole himself.

As we have just shown, any halfheartedness gives rise to *anxiety*. This is why it is a mark of the philistine, especially the cultural philistine, who knows only what he has learned but does not know himself. (Cause and effect can be interchanged, or can form a vicious circle.) When Freud ascertains that the ego is the true seat of fear, this is due to the one-sidedness, or limitedness, of consciousness, described above. Anxiety is related to the Latin *angustiae*, which means "restrictedness." When we are frightened, we are also fascinated by our fear (vicious circle). This is shown, for example, in the fear of evil spirits, the spell of fear or, in modern times, by nightmares.

Jung once gave an account of a French officer who had chosen a military career out of fear. This did not have the desired effect, the anxiety remained, and so he decided to become a Trappist monk. Later he became a Cistercian and went to Africa as a missionary, where he maintained his vow of silence, lived as a vegetarian and worked in the fields. He was finally killed by the natives. As the defense mechanisms were inappropriate, the source of his fear was forced to take concrete form and thus claim its victim; for fear is an inverted (reciprocal) yearning for the feared objective. This can be seen very clearly in the spell of fear, an example of which we shall quote here:

> Should the lover of a servant or a pregnant whore have run off, then a certain penny is placed in the little pan of a mill; the mill is set going and gathers speed and the one who has fled becomes so afraid that he comes scurrying home. That is called "putting fear into someone."[38]

The return of the one who has fled, brought about by casting a spell that creates fear, amounts to a restoration of wholeness, with the rotation of the mill symbolizing the circle.

The "normal" person usually holds his own against fear by managing to devalue the object of the fear through his equilibrium. At the beginning of our century, this heroic approach culminated in Freud's psychoanalysis where, for example, the attempt was made to devaluate sexuality by "exposing" it as "nothing but" a matter of course and the most natural thing in the world, and therefore not "entitled" to cause anxiety. This "nothing but" argument was "exposed" by W. James (1842-1910) as medical materialism.[39] The way this works with Freud is in the reduction of the *fascinosum* (cf. Rudolf Otto) to incompatible desires of an infantile nature. Religion, of course, is also affected by this judgment. Some years ago two American psychologists ascertained that the students of a religious group had more manifest anxiety than those of a non-religious segment of the population.[40] But where would the human race be without *tremendum* (cf. p. 26: "To feel the thrill of awe

---

[38] Jacob Grimm, *German Mythology*, Original German version: *Deutsche Mythologie*, Gütersloh 1877.
[39] William James, *Varieties of Religious Experience*, London, 1890.

crowns man's creation")? A. Adler also tried the same trick, with reduction to infantile craving for recognition, albeit not without hitting on a far-reaching problem.

In contrast it must be said that anxiety exists only where something "quite different" is not given its full due but at the same time is not necessarily repressed. This gives rise, for example, to the problem of the emotional relationship between the two sexes (Chapters IX and X). Of course we are not referring to real fear here, as when one is attacked by an assailant, but to that sort of fear by which one is actually fascinated. Transitions, such as the fear of enemy nations, for example, should not be denied. We would not wish to give the impression that it is a simple matter to overcome the fear of what looks like such an alien opposite. On the whole, it is easier to follow Mephistopheles' advice and confine oneself to an average existence:

> There is a means, and it requires not gold
> Magic or medicine; away with you
> Into the fields – begin to hew and delve –
> Confine yourself, and limit every wish
> Within a narrow circle – feed upon
> Meats, simple, undisguised – and live, in short,
> Beast-like, 'mong beasts – deem it no degradation
> Thyself to spread the dung upon the field,
> The growth of which thou art to reap – this is
> Indeed the best way to repair life's powers,
> And wear at eighty a hale countenance.
>
> *Faust I,* "Witch's Kitchen"

In such a "narrow circle," the four functions would all more or less have the same value, as is the case with so-called primitives, and with the corresponding unconsciousness, of course, the tensions of opposites would more or less cease completely.

So a large part of humankind can remain content with things as they seem to be. In fact one might say that the "normal person" contents himself with whatever obtains at the time. This leads to the decisive question of whether the "normal person" is in fact the one who is not content? The next logical step, and we have no qualms about taking it,

---

[40] Arthur M. Adlerstein and E. Alexander Irving, *The Relationship between Religious Belief and Negative Affect toward Death.* 66 Annual Convention of APA, Washington D.C. 1958.

is to state that we are inclined to regard the neurotic person and the creative person as normal. This brings us to the type of sudden change brought about through a breakthrough of unconscious contents.

Neurotic people suffer from symptoms which, similar to dreams, are entitled to be considered as the spontaneous expressions of the reverse side of the unconscious. In this sense they represent the sufferings of this person in a normal way. Strictly speaking, a discussion of this nature belongs to the sphere of psychopathology. We mention it here because the contents of these spontaneous expressions can be "creative" in the sense that they show a tendency toward wholeness. In modern times we often come across such people, who claim that what they produce in this way is normal.

In another case, however, creative people want to create a different world, and they fight a heroic battle on its behalf; in other words, they actively accept their suffering. In both cases the disturbances caused by the unconscious can be very similar. The difference is that the neurotic fights against it in his fear, whereas the creative person is fascinated by it and welcomes it. The boundaries are by no means easy to see; for on the one hand, modern art has great difficulty in accepting the ugly and the infantile (inferior function), and on the other hand, when the inferior is accepted, it is left in the primeval state, magnanimously declared to be great (*fascinosum*).

By way of contrast, a truly creative achievement is the painstaking processing of raw material from the unconsciousness. As with any birth, a true work of art is preceded by labor pains. We could quote Nietzsche to show these labor pains of the creative:

> It was my hardest and sickest winter (1882/83), apart from 10 days, which just sufficed for me to do something for the sake of which my whole hard and sick existence is worthwhile.
>
> – (Letters on Zarathustra)[41]

It should not be forgotten that the creative is the heroic. It is a way of the Cross, vividly represented in Dürer's copper engraving "Knight, Death and Devil."

We come now to change toward wholeness through a traumatic disturbance. Among the traumatic disturbances of the differentiated function, we wish to include all cases in which a breakdown occurs in

[41] trans. D.R.

the face of a problem for which the previously held attitude proves totally inadequate. It may take a long time before the person realizes that a total change is the only answer, and that this change may take the form of a depression and may call for medical assistance.

In contrast to changes brought about more by external factors, there are those that come purely from within. This is where we particularly find the failure of the main function, which has run dry. What then happens is that pious people start to have doubts, active people become weary, and young people are disappointed with the world or disappointed in love, for example.

As examples I would like to mention a painter who was commissioned to decorate a church wall and a baritone singer who suddenly lost his splendid voice. The painter's subject matter was "The pouring out of the Holy Spirit." He was an intuitive type, and as he was doing the painting he was so overwhelmed by the unconscious that the church wall was no longer large enough and he had to abandon the project. He never gave much thought to what he had felt and so his magnum opus was never completed. As for the singer, careful investigation revealed that he was having awful marriage problems, and that he was doing his best to avoid thinking about them.

If we consider what theoretical conclusions we can draw from what we have said so far about the phenomenology of the functions and attitudes, then the following points can be made:

1. Between the main function (consciousness) and the inferior function (unconscious) there is a sort of all-or-none reaction (the exclusion principle).
2. In this relationship the inferior function (unconscious) enjoys a great degree of autonomy over consciousness.
3. The inferior function has compensatory significance for the conscious in that it always completes the image.
4. However, there is also a complementary relationship between the conscious and the unconscious, insofar as both aspects are indispensable to acquiring wholeness, regardless of how much they seem to contradict one another.
5. As a consequence of points 3 and 4, the unconscious is theoretically in a position to transform the personality, by indicating the necessary changes and suggesting a new alternative toward wholeness.

6. On the level of the collective conscious, the alternative paths are expressed in myths, religions and holy mysteries.

The objective of the following chapters of this book is to make clear what form the phenomenology of such a process usually adopts.

Chapter V

Figures of the Road to Individuation

After the appearance of his typology book (1921), C.G. Jung published very little else on the subject. In actual analytical sessions, typological problems were seldom discussed, yet it was still important to him as the *compass* we have just been talking about. Of course, the spontaneous development of personality must never be squeezed into a mold, and the analyst has to tread very warily in this respect. We have seen only too often what happens when people are indoctrinated to the point that they fit neatly into the preconceived theory of the observer. For reasons already mentioned, there is no easy way of giving a documentary presentation of this developmental process. Each individual case would fill volumes, and psychologists would still come along and say, with justification, that the individual case proves nothing.

But in such developmental processes there is a particular phenomenon that is rather common, and this aroused Jung's curiosity. He first wrote about it in 1929, after having read a commentary to an ancient Chinese alchemistic text, dating back to the 8th century, translated by R. Wilhelm and bearing the title *The Secret of the Golden Flower*.[42] In the graphic representations discussed here, which came into existence in the analytical process, Jung once again encountered the quaternio.

There were striking similarities between these representations and certain Indian cultic images, and this led Jung to give them the name mandala, which is Sanskrit for "circle." Clinical observation revealed that this could only be a symbolic expression of the objective in the personality development of the analysand. Jung had already given this

---

[42]R. Wilhelm, *The Secret of the Golden Flower*; a Chinese book of Life. Translated and explained by Richard Wilhelm, with a foreword and commentary by C.G. Jung. Trans. from German by Cary F. Baynes, Revised ed. London and New York, 1962.

development a name – the individuation process. Hence, any patterns resembling mandalas may be regarded as symbols of this objective.

As a "substitute" for statistical documentation, Jung had already made use of the amplification method in dream interpretation (cf. Vol. 2 of this textbook series, p. 7 ff.). The section on cultural history in his typology book is an example of the amplification method. The mandala-like paintings of his analysands, however, and the confrontation with the quaternio as the fundamental structure of the psyche, led Jung in new directions; until almost the end of his days, he felt compelled to devote all his efforts to establishing the proof of the universal importance of this motif, using amplificatory examples from the history of civilization. Alchemistic literature, which he had already discovered in the text of the *Golden Flower,* proved to be a rich vein in this respect. The reader is well advised to keep these connections in mind when looking at the results of Jung's study of numerous original works.

The huge amount of amplificatory material Jung brought to light makes it clear that individuation is a matter of concern for the whole of humankind. What he originally discovered in the analytical process is generally true – actually a law of nature. We seem to be born with this objective, and its symbolic expression, the quaternio, is thus actually an archetype. The process comes to the fore more clearly in the analytical process. People who go into analysis have a greater intensity than so-called healthy people because of their symptoms, but the pressure comes from the unconscious. This is probably why the average person follows it blindly or at most vaguely suspecting what might be going on. Only a few people will consciously accept the responsibility for the process that their life is undergoing. They live it or are lived by it or are simply driven by it, instead of experiencing it. When the unconscious demands consciousness, i.e., develops symptoms, for example, then there is always much-praised good will and common sense that enables us to deny it and to boast about our willpower. The breakthrough is thus "successfully" foiled. Today there are scores of "schools" that help us to steer clear of the symptoms. I would be extremely wary of every one of them unless they take into account the relationship between "healing" and "wholeness," because they may cheat us of wholeness in the service of losing the symptoms, i.e., the "elimination" of the unconscious.

The small minority of people who are seriously prepared to take the unconscious into consideration and to embark upon the dangerous path (see Figure 5, p. 57) are conscious of the individuation process. This means they will experience it with greater intensity and consequently will adapt better to the external and internal conditions of life. When an active participation in the conflict between the conscious and the unconscious becomes apparent in the acceleration of the individuation process (usually through paying attention to dreams), we gain more living time to make our growing wholeness beneficial not only for ourselves, but for our relationships with our fellowmen and the world around us.

We shall now attempt to outline the phenomenology of the developmental process of the personality toward wholeness). However, on no account must the impression arise that this is a rule or prescription that must be adhered to. The infiniteness of nature unfailingly ensures variations of all kinds, and this must be respected. The pattern of the four functions and the two attitudes is intended merely to provide the observer with guidelines.

Before we proceed, we must recapitulate certain fundamental prerequisites from the first three volumes of this textbook series.

1. It is questionable whether it is possible to give a straightforward definition of consciousness. We shall simply state that consciousness is a field full of many contents and equipped with the four basic functions. It can be described functionally as a reference system, the center of which is the ego or ego complex, with the latter predominantly geared to the object (extroverted) or to the subject (introverted). Its energetic aspect is the will.

2. By way of contrast, the term unconscious is a "limit" concept in the Kantian sense, and we shall use the term in his negative definition to "limit the arrogance of sensuousness." What this means for us is simply that the phenomena of consciousness by no means exhaust the sphere of the psyche. Thus the term is a genuine *noumenon*, i.e., something that can be "the object only of pure reason," which cannot be apprehended by 'theoretical dogma' *(noumenorum non datur scientia),* but only by 'practical dogma.'[43] This may become clearer if we give Kant's definition of the phenomena (contents of consciousness) as the opposite of the *noumena:* they are "the cate-

---

[43] I. Kant, *Critique of Pure Reason.* Trans. by Norman Kemp Smith, London and New York, 1929.

gorically conceived sensory objects, i.e., manifestations, insofar as
they are conceived as objects according to the unity of the categories."

If the unconscious is really unconscious then neither its contents nor
its functions can be actually experienced. Only when the conscious
interferes with the unconscious do recognizable phenomena emerge.
These are themselves contents of the conscious, but cannot be explained
solely in these terms, for they appear alien to the ego. They are
experienced as intruders because one does not know where they come
from. If one assumes that they come from the unconscious, then they
can help us draw conclusions about its contents. As a rule, these strange
contents also contain familiar elements; in fact they can have the
appearance of deriving entirely from the conscious. What is strange
about them is, for example, a curious linking up of motifs or an
unusually emotional effect. When we are sometimes able to identify
these contents as such, coming from the conscious, then they are
"specifically" altered, and it is this very alteration that enables us to
draw conclusions about the essence of the unconscious.

The best known spontaneously occurring examples of this interaction between the conscious and the unconscious are dreams. In them we
find "remnants of the day" which, with slight variations, can be traced
back to contents of the conscious. On the other hand, many dream
contents are specifically modulated, and have, for example, fantastical,
archaic and primitive characteristics. In the dream we are with these
contents in a primeval world, and thus become primeval beings (cf. Vol.
2).[44] This is as good a reason as any for not identifying oneself as such
with the self in the dream. The dream is a classical example of the
influence of the unconscious on the conscious.

$$\text{Conscious} \quad \overset{1}{\underset{2}{\rightleftarrows}} \quad \text{Unconscious}$$

This influence is unlikely to be only one-way (1), but is probably
reciprocal, so that the conscious also affects the unconscious (2). For
example, the supposition has been clinically proven that, for example,

[44] Cf. Vol. 2 of this textbook series.

when the conscious works on dreams in the analytical situation, this then has repercussions on the contents and processes produced by the unconscious. This supports the theory of the presence of a reciprocal effect. One is tempted to think of a chemical reaction, such as $2\,H+O = H_2O$, where, for example, H represents an unconscious content, O represents consciousness, and the product (H_2O) is a totally new material which, without analysis, would seem to have none of the properties of the elements or components. In other words, both systems change when they interact.

A further consequence of the above observations is that it cannot be a matter of indifference what one dreams, for it certainly matters what happens to our consciousness. The third logical consequence is that one ought to pay attention to one's dreams. As early as the 4th century, Synesius was recommending that we keep "night journals" rather than conventional diaries (cf. Vol. 2, p. 64).

A large sample of dream material has revealed the following information: most dreams consist of *images*. If these are interpreted in terms of "specific modulations" in relation to the consciousness contents, then certain regular features begin to emerge.

1. Images have common characteristics as regards the specific dream contents.
2. They also often have typical dream situations, such as flying, falling, anxiety, paralysis, and so on, and this has given rise to a corresponding classification of dreams.[45]
3. There are typical dream figures ("people").
4. In lengthy dream series, regular successions of dream situations and figures can be seen, a point to which we shall return later.

With the above points it is always necessary to bear in mind the dreamer's real life situation and his state of consciousness. This means that alongside the dream text we also have the so-called context, as well as the dreamer's associations.

Jung directed his attention especially to dream figures and situations, and over a period of time he began to see definable constants in such images and processes, which correlated very positively with the real life or consciousness situations of the dreamer concerned. For this he

[45] Compare: K. Leonhard, *Die Gesetze des normalen Träumens*, Leipzig 1939.

coined the term "archetypal images," which we shall talk about later. Another point to which we shall return is the perception that dream contents and processes regularly have a compensatory function in relation to the prevailing state of consciousness.

A final observation of Jung's, important for us in connection with the subject matter of this book, is the following: if one consciously and consistently pays attention to one's dream contents (as in analysis, for example), then one can see a chronological, more or less ordered sequence in them. This in turn has an effect on the process of the development of consciousness – what Jung called the individuation process.

This dynamic between the conscious and the unconscious shows us that unless an individual participates in it he remains "unconscious." Such a person sticks rigidly to what is already known and familiar and clings firmly to consciousness. In refusing to become aware of all the other factors at work within him, i.e., his unconscious, he remains unconscious of it all. We refer to a person's "unconsciousness," which can be misleading, if not paradoxical, for what it means is actually a tenacious clinging to consciousness.

On the subject of consciousness, let us now recapitulate: first, consciousness is perceiving oneself in relation to one surroundings. If I relate the surroundings to myself, this is called reflection. In other words what I do is perceive what goes on *within me* through my experience of the outside world. If I look at it more critically I then discover the "subjective factor." This, however, is only on condition that I do not naively identify or even hypostatize the image" with the concrete and actual facts or data, as was the case in the famous example of the Enkekalymmenos (veiled man) from the field of Logic. The Megarian philosopher Eubulides used this as an illustration of a fallacy: the pupil is asked the question, "Can you recognize your father?" Answer: "Yes." Second question: "Can you recognize this veiled man?" Answer: "No." He is then told that the veiled man is his father, that he can thus recognize him and not recognize him.

The "subjective factor" comes from the inner world and with it our definition of consciousness as a perceiving of oneself in relation to one's surroundings becomes inadequate. But the inner world is an unconscious prerequisite for all our perceiving and functioning. Once again experience shows here that this unconscious prerequisite is in a compensatory relationship to consciousness. And here, too, the dictum applies that it cannot be a matter of indifference whether or not the conscious comes to terms with the unconscious.

Let us take another look at the empirically corroborated differences between the conscious and the unconscious: the conscious is intermittent, individually historically variant, is of a personal nature and is individual, whereas the unconscious is continuous, individually historically invariant, impersonal (or at best partially personal) and collective, unless it is the "personal unconscious," which is on the borderline between the two systems. Once again we are reminded of Heraclitus (fr. 89 B), which recalls the individuality of the inner world of the sleeper. This inner world is certainly "individual," often peculiar, strange and not only "private" but often quite impersonal. As an example of the peculiarity of the inner world of dreams, here is a dream of a woman about 40 years old:

> I was looking after an infant baby while his teacher was being told about the conscious and the unconscious. Then I am the one who explains it. The teacher had placed the baby not at the bottom of the class but as 0.1289th. I found this stupid. The baby talked to me very intelligently even though he was only 6 or 7 months old.
>
> Then along came a little horse with someone on its back who was riding it very badly, his backside stuck in the air, frantically trying to restrain the horse by holding the reins too short, which only made the horse gallop even faster. It made me laugh.

The baby that talks, goes to school, is given this odd ranking by the teacher, the teacher who has to learn! (the difference between conscious and unconscious), the horse that gallops more quickly the more it is restrained – all of these are unfamiliar, impersonal figures, and thus are all typical dream elements.

The fact that the unconscious is different should not blind us to the similarities, because most dream contents are *anthropomorphous*. *Canis panem somniat, piscator pisces* recalls the everyday preoccupations that fill our dreams, and thus Freud's remnants of the day. Yet one must be careful not to automatically trace back dream contents to the familiar and everyday. It would be a euhemerism to make a principle of it. Euhemeros (4th B.C.) was a Cyrenaic and disciple of Aristippos and lived at the court of the Macedonian King Cassandros. In his writings, only fragments of which have survived, he puts forward the theory that the gods of mythology were originally heroic mortals who were worshiped and revered because of their great achievements. We learn more

about this from Cicero[46] and Minucius Felix.[47] This rationalistic theory
for the rise of religion as a result of conscious intent and reflection is
referred to as euhemerism. Since Euhemeros, a rationalism related to
physics has also come into being; it is closely related to the development of the natural sciences and claims that religion stems from a
reinterpretation of natural manifestations. A third rationalistic theory is
a psychological one and views concepts of god as conscious self-
externalizations of human characteristics. In contrast to these three
attitudes there are also anti-rationalistic theories, which declare that
religion is a thing in itself; in other words, that it is an autocthonous
function of the human soul, the thing that is specifically human.

It is a well-known fact that Freud advocates a psychologically
rational euhemerism; this is evident in his early work, *Totem and Taboo*
(1913) and more so in *The Future of an Illusion* (1928).[48] In the first of
these treatises the presumed father is viewed in a purely personal and
negative light, but this does not explain why and to what end this
negative idolization occurs, for it is simply an obstacle to the son's
development. With Freud at any rate, the "father" is in no way viewed
as an autochthonous factor in one's soul. Let us not forget to point out
here that the negative attitude of young men towards the personal father
(and mother!) is perhaps a necessary thing if they are not to be idolized;
this would be a fatal error, but in the godlessness of the age we are living
in it is unfortunately a distinct possibility.

However, if we are to understand dreams and myths as "dreams of
mankind," then the question of why and for what purpose, and hence
the question of the finality of the contents of the unconscious, become
crucial ones and give these contents a meaning in their own right. If we
allow their effect, then this would make the final aspect undoubtedly
more important than the purely causal one.

We can learn much more from these contents if we regard them as
personified complexes or partial personalities (cf. Vols. 1 and 2 of this
textbook series), because closer investigation of such figures shows us
that they can acquire their personality character only on the basis of an
underlying wholeness. We must not forget that the idea of compensa-

---

[46] Cicero, de nat. Deor. I. 42, 119.
[47] Minucius Felix, Oct. 20, 4 and 21, 1.
[48] S. Freud, *Totem and Taboo*, trans. by James Strachey. Standard Edition, Vol.
13 (1955), and *The Future of an Illusion*. Standard Edition, Vol. 21 (1961).

tion (compensatory relationship between contents of the conscious and the unconscious) subsumes a higher wholeness, or an authority that seeks wholeness.

This fact emerges particularly clearly in the course of the individuation process, which has a distinctive autonomy. This autonomy is seen in the activity of our dream figures (our partial personalities), which frequently act in contradiction to our conscious intentions and views. As we stated in Vol. 1 of this textbook series, this autonomy can already be seen in the complexes, which, for the same reason, have a tendency toward *personification*. In this they follow the principle of the similarity and difference between the contents of the conscious and the contents of the unconscious. If we think of this personification as one of the most striking peculiarities of dreams, let us just recall their fairy-tale and legend-like quality, or the occasional appearance of chimeras, which we should not explain away reductively, but rather should understand as specific factors of the world of the unconscious. For if we attempt to trace them back to the known and the familiar, then we have to introduce another dimension, one which is accountable to reality for change. However, because it is not evident why a thing that is consciously clear should be expressed so unclearly, Freud felt compelled to introduce another dimension – censorship – to support his *petitio principii*. This contradicts the axiom known as Occam's razor, which states that explanatory principles should not be multiplied beyond the necessary (*entia non sunt multiplicanda praeter necessitatem*). Although censorship is also a "higher" authority, it derives from the conscious and is extremely negative. So that it shall nevertheless have a positive sense, it has been given the function of watching over sleep. There is, however, no support for this hypothesis in modern experimental sleep and dream research.

It is much less complicated to go along with Jung in the assumption that the dream says exactly what it means without beating about the bush, even if it doesn't suit us at all, which is quite often the case. The conscious already nurtures more than enough prejudices as it is, and we can only be grateful if dreams try to get rid of them. Of course, this is once again a compensatory function so that with this argument, as above, we are again forced to assume that there is a higher authority, a preexisting wholeness that asserts itself in our dreams.

The peculiarity of the unconscious material is usually particularly striking in pathological cases. Early on with Jung we find the example of the "solar phallus."[49] An uneducated paranoidal patient, who had been interned for years in the Burghölzli, the Psychiatric Clinic of the University of Zürich, described one of his hallucinations to a Dr. Honegger. He said that he could see an erect phallus on the sun and that when he moved his head from side to side, the sun's phallus moved with it, and that was where the wind came from. It was only much later, in his mythological studies, that Jung came across a Greek text published by Albrecht Dieterich under the title *Eine Mithrasliturgie* (1903).[50] On pages 7 and 8 there is, word for word, an identical vision of a solar phallus as the source of the wind. It can be safely assumed that the patient had no knowledge of this myth. The fact that a mythological concept was spontaneously replicated from the (sick) soul of the patient was a crucial step in leading Jung to the supposition of the existence of a collective unconscious. This supposition was confirmed more and more by his growing experience with the material of the unconscious on the one hand, and with mythological material on the other. The amazing parallelism of the two visions, even to the tiniest detail, will have to suffice for the purpose of our observations. But this does not tell us what the motif meant for the patient, which it is no longer possible to know. I knew the patient personally and have his casebook, which is over 200 pages long, but so far I have never succeeded in finding out the function of the solar phallus in his hallucination system. During my time he no longer remembered it and his system was producing fewer and fewer fantasies, a condition euphemistically known as "schizophrenic dementia."

In healthy people it can be seen that such archaic contents are firmly blocked out and only emerge occasionally through inexplicable *affects*. When, for no apparent reason, we "see red" or become emotional, closer investigation may reveal this as an intervention from such unconscious images. One form of investigation would be the Association Experiment (cf. Vol. 1 of this textbook series). These images are primitive, archaic and first and foremost betray a specific difficulty in adapting to external reality. As none of us is immune from such "break-

---

[49] C.G. Jung, Symbols of Transformation, CW 5. German original, 1911 and 1912.
[50] Albrecht Dieterich, *Eine Mithrasliturgie*, Leipzig 1903. (Reprint of the 3rd edn. Leipzig and Berlin 1923) 1966. Trans. by G.R.S. Mead: *A Mithraic Ritual*, London and Benares 1907.

ins," in the course of our cultural development, we have built up a series of safety devices, for example, in the form of a code of good behavior.

Such contents may be regarded as *relics* on the one hand, but also as potential for future development on the other. We must never forget that in this sense the unconscious has a Janus head. On the one hand it is the preconscious, even prehistoric, world of instinct, and on the other hand it is also our future on the basis of instincts that are ready to spring into action. This explains the archaic and historic aspects of its contents. The contents of the unconscious can be understood in the former case as effects of the world of instinct, and in the latter as the purpose of this readiness to come to the fore. As we mentioned earlier, this presupposes such a thing as a personality in the unconscious, which in turn explains its autonomy in relation to the conscious (cf. Vol. 1) and is a point in favor of collaboration between the conscious and the unconscious.

Chapter VI

Phenomenology of Individuation

In the course of acquiring his vast wealth of experience, Jung was forced to assume that from the depths of our unconscious there is a superior personality addressing us. To be on the safe side, one would probably have to say that when one does not simply analyze the manifestations of the unconscious reductively, i.e., by not only reducing them to what is already known and familiar, but rather allowing them a final significance, then a higher authority begins to emerge that is superordinate to the combined entity of consciousness and unconsciousness. In other words, a center appears on the scene that embraces the total personality (consciousness and unconscious). Jung gave this center the term *self*. It tends to crystallize slowly in the course of the development of the personality, and then develops more rapidly in response to what happens when the conscious actively comes to terms with the unconscious. Jung first gave (fragmentary) statistics of this phenomenon in his 1935 Eranos lecture, entitled "Dream Symbols of the Individuation Process."[51] The material of the same dreamer is dealt with more thoroughly in *Psychology and Alchemy*.[52]

Our aim in this chapter is to describe the phenomena that tend to occur in the process of personality development in the analytical situation. Of course, it is not possible to neatly delineate what actually happens when the conscious tries to come to terms with the unconscious. Our assumption of a certain sequence in this process must be seen only as the outline of an average example of events in the individuation process. We do not explicitly make use of the typological schema here, because the typological differences manifest themselves only in the individual shaping of the archetypal *figures,* and not in the

[51] C.G. Jung, *Dream Symbols of the Individuation Process* in the Eranos-Jahrbuch, 1935. (Now Part II of Psychology and Alchemy).
[52] C.G. Jung, *Psychology and Alchemy*, CW 12, 1953.

way they actually behave. Furthermore, in Chapter III we already discussed the sequence in which the *functions* can be integrated.

The Shadow

We shall now examine the phenomenology of a typical dream figure that can frequently be observed in the early stages of analysis. At an early stage, figures often appear in dreams that the dreamer dislikes and may feel unfriendly toward, or even hostile. Bearing in mind what we said in Vol. 2 of this textbook series about the subjective level, then these attitudes can only be the dreamer's negative projections. It is common knowledge that each of us has at least one such *bête noire* in his vicinity, so this is a common human problem. This is why it has found expression in the most ancient national customs. One custom that is well-known is the ancient Jewish scapegoat ritual, in which an expiatory sacrifice is part of the Day of Atonement.[53] A goat is laden with the sins of the people, driven into the desert and thus sacrificed to the Azazel. In his monumental work *The Golden Bough,* Sir J.G. Frazer has devoted a whole volume, entitled "The Scapegoat," to this universal motif.[54] In Switzerland one of many examples would be the "Posterli-Jagd" in the Entlebuch.[55] All these rites become urgent as the darkness grows, that is, toward the end of the year, and call for a renewal of the weakened light principle, which risks being overwhelmed by darkness and hence by evil. In Christianity the appearance of the new God (baby) is celebrated with lights (Christmas tree) at the darkest time of the year, and Christ is celebrated as the *Agnus Dei, qui tollit peccata mundi.*

For such figures, Jung chose the more neutral term of *shadow* rather than "scapegoats." Given that Jung's expressions for certain typical dream figures and motifs are not terms as such, but merely collective names for phenomena with certain similarities, we shall dispense with definitions. Instead we shall attempt to describe the classical features of each of these images and thus shall seek to find an explanation for the phenomenon.

[53] Levit. 8, 1-21 and 16, 20-22.
[54] J.G. Frazer, *The Golden Bough,* Vol VI, London 1914.
[55] Cf. E. Hoffmann-Krayer, *Feste und Bräuche des Schweizervolkes,* Zürich 1949, p. 81.

We have a certain view or image of ourselves and we try to believe in this, or at least we want those around us to believe in it. As a result, we take care to ensure that the darker side of this image remains in the dark. We would hate to be confused with our "dark brother," and we ourselves do not want to know anything about him, so we avoid the mirror or deceive ourselves into thinking that the dark side of the mirror image is not there.

In using a visual form of expression to describe a dream figure as a shadow, it will be clear that it must be the same sex as the dreamer. Moreover, because the shadow bears one or several tabooed characteristics, it thereby gives rise to emotional reactions. We are very wary of people maliciously touching our shadows. Recall that among many so-called primitives it is regarded as a serious offense, and even a dangerous one for the guilty party, if someone treads on another's (real) shadow. One can thus safely assume that such figures embody aspects of the inferior function.

Understanding a shadow figure on the subjective level presents a considerable problem, for the image is then binding! This is tremendously difficult if it is a thief or a murderer, for example. Think of the case of a thoroughly respectable woman who, when she is at this stage, constantly dreams about prostitutes, alcoholics or drug addicts. When we were talking about typology, we said that the inferior function is part of the whole. Being compensatory to the main function, it is initially incompatible, but in the course of the individuation process it becomes differentiated and thereby acceptable. Anyone who does not cast a shadow is not a real (material) person, unless he is a saint, for in Persia, for example, saints do not have shadows (like Mohammed), and in Ancient Greece, anyone who entered the Abaton of Zeus on the Lykaion lost his shadow. However, such places no doubt no longer exist. If we lose our shadow, this actually means that we have lost our humanity. The devil has no shadow, which is why he buys it from Peter Schlemil, thus making the shadow the devil's fee.[56] Let us also recall the *Spiegelmensch* trilogy by Franz Werfel (1920). In both works we see an attempt at special, if not very successful, solutions to the shadow problem. One should also bear in mind that the "bush soul" of the primitive is closely connected to our question and that primitives handle it with extreme caution, because they are fully aware of its dangerous

[56] A. von Chamisso, *Peter Schlemils wundersame Geschichte*. 1814.

side. The "blood brotherhood" with the devil, the epitome of absolute evil, is thus under any circumstances a destructive solution.[57]

Shadow figures in dreams usually have a rather odd dual aspect, in that they are half personal and half impersonal. The impersonal aspect tells us that there are elements of the collective unconscious in the shadow. An impressive example of this is a dream of Hannibal's that Cicero recounts:

> After the conquest of Sagunt, Hannibal saw himself in a dream where he was being summoned by Jupiter to the Council of the Gods. On his arrival, Jupiter commanded him to wage war on Italy and provided him with an escort from the Council. Accompanied by this escort, he set off marching with his army. His leader, however, warned him not to turn round, but finally his curiosity got the better of him and he did turn round. What he saw was a terrible monstrous animal, with serpents woven round its body, which was destroying crops, bushes and houses with every step that it took. In amazement he asked his divine escort what this monster signified. Back came the reply: "Italy's ruin!" with the admonition not to waste time and not to bother about what was going on behind his back.[58]

As can be seen, the negative side of Hannibal's heroic deeds is hot on his heels, and has super- or subhuman mythological dimensions.

Let us look at some other dreams, more personal examples, beginning with a short, simple preanalytical dream of a middle-aged man:

> I am standing on a raft in the river Limmat in Zürich. Next to me a policeman pulls out a net in which there is a young man; his face looks like mine but it is dark and blurred. He is alive.

A dream of a young man as an example of a dream in the early stages of analysis:

> I am helping F. to empty his cupboard because he wants to go home. F. is loaded up and overburdened with all sorts of objects. I help him to carry some of them out. But I can see that he will never make it home with all this stuff. More than half of his things are balloon-like. I suggest letting the air out of all of them and rolling them up. Then he would have room in his cases.

---

[57] Cf. E. Rudolph, Teufelsbündner im 20. Jahrhundert, in Schweiz. Arch. f. Volkskunde, 72, 1-2, Basel 1976, pp. 33-54.
[58] Cicero, de divin. I.24.

The dreamer had a negative effect on F. He calls him an inflated artist, indulging in fantasies and not doing anything properly. F. is newly married, introverted; the dreamer is unmarried and extroverted. On the subjective level, F. is one of the dreamer's shadow figures, on which are projected all the supposed negative characteristics of the subject. The balloons indicate inflation, which in this case means that although F. does have creative qualities, he doesn't do anything about them except fantasize. This projection is only half true so long as the subject is left aside. But this is where it begins to become difficult to understand this other world, which is the dreamer's unconscious. In Chapter IV of *Psychological Types,* Jung made it clear how the intro-verted author of a book he was discussing[59] presents a completely unfair picture of the extrovert and also an inadequate one of the author's own (introverted) type.

The following example gives us an opportunity to discuss further important aspects of the shadow problem.

> I was sent abroad as a spy. A former prisoner recognizes and betrays me. I am pursued and have to escape over the rooftops and break windows in order to get away, and have to use a pistol to defend myself. Then I am able to escape down a chimney and get really black, but I get a job as a chimney sweeper's assistant and so nobody recognizes me and I am safe.

Here the dreamer is "commanded" to investigate the enemy, his dark side (shadow). The shadow recognizes him but does not wish to be recognized itself and pursues him (dangers of the unconscious). Thus he is forced to go into the dark *himself.* From his own body he learns that intellectual acknowledgment alone does not suffice. The dire situation represents a vital need to deal with the dark, which is what actually happens on a professional basis (chimney sweeper). This is in contrast to the normal situation, when our inferior side appears only when we let ourselves go, when something stupid happens, or when we catch ourselves doing something nasty. The hitherto unlived life, this alter ego, this unreliable, possibly even rebellious, dark brother now has to learn to be active in a useful way. In doing so he will cease to be a threat.

This shows us clearly the *ambivalence* of the shadow, for it is not just a negative thing but can be very useful if dealt with properly. This

---

[59] Furneaux Jordan, *Character as seen in Body and Parentage*, London 1896.

ambivalence is especially noticeable in young people, where qualities
that might be of value are often incorporated into the shadow, but go to
waste because external reasons prevent these values from being nur-
tured and lived. We know that ambivalence is part of the essence of
every symbol, which means that the shadow can be described as a
symbol. The symbol always unites in itself two contradictory sides. The
symbolic nature of the shadow can be seen most clearly in its variation
of the *doppelgänger* or *double*. Drugs, which can be both a poison and
a remedy, also have this symbolic character. We are reminded here of
the *Rubáiyát of Omar Khayyam,* the 11th century Persian poet, mathematician and astronomer, where it says:

> If a sage hands you poison, drink it. If a fool hands you the antidote, pour
> it out.[60]

Any discussion on the shadow inevitably brings up the awkward
problem of *Good and Evil,* and the relativity of the two dimensions. One
example, the 18th Sura of the Koran, is so good we shall quote it at
length:

> They found one of Our servants to whom We had vouchsafed Our mercy
> and whom We had endowed with knowledge of Our own. Moses said to
> him: "May I follow you so that you may guide me by that which you have
> been taught?"
> "You will not bear with me," replied the other. "For how can you bear
> with that which is beyond your knowledge?"
> Moses said: "If Allah wills, you shall find me patient: I shall not in
> anything disobey you."
> He said: "If you are bent on following me, you must ask no question about
> anything until I myself speak to you concerning it."
> The two set forth, but as soon as they embarked, Moses companion bored
> a hole in the bottom of the ship.
> "A strange thing you have done!" exclaimed Moses. "Is it to drown her
> passengers that you have bored a hole in her?"
> "Did I not tell you," he replied, "that you would not bear with me?"
> "Pardon my forgetfulness," said Moses. "Do not be angry with me on
> account of this."
> They journeyed on until they fell in with a certain youth. Moses' compan-
> ion slew him, and Moses said: "You have killed an innocent man who has
> done no harm. Surely you have committed a wicked crime."

[60] Omar Khayyam, Rubáiyát LIII.

"Did I not tell you," he replied, "that you would not bear with me?"

Moses said: "If ever I question you again, abandon me; for then I should deserve it."

They travelled on until they came to a certain city. They asked the people for some food, but they declined to receive them as their guests. There they found a wall on the point of falling down. His companion restored it, and Moses said: "Had you wished, you could have demanded payment for your labors."

"Now has the time arrived when we must part," said the other. "But first I will explain to you those acts of mine which you could not bear to watch with patience.

Know that the ship belonged to some poor fishermen. I damaged it because in their rear there was a king who was taking every ship by force.

As for the youth, his parents both are true believers, and we feared lest he should plague them with his wickedness and unbelief. It was our wish that their Lord should grant them another in his place, a son more righteous and more filial.

As for the wall, it belonged to two orphan boys in the city whose father was an honest man. Beneath it their treasure is buried. Your Lord decreed in His mercy that they should dig out their treasure when they grew to manhood. What I did was not done by my will.

That is the meaning of what you could not bear to watch with patience."[61]

We find here several examples of the meaning of "Evil"; i.e., evil here becomes a "doctrine," which reminds us of the *beata culpa* and the *mysterium iniquitas* of the Church. At any rate, this doctrine is a more satisfactory one than that of the *privatio boni,* according to which evil is nothing more than an omission of good. Wilhelm Busch wrote something along the same lines that is much more acceptable:

> The good – and this is really true –
> Is just the evil you do not do.[62]

We are still being told today that *omne bonum a Deo, omne malum ab homine* (all good is derived from God, all wickedness from man), but the Old Testament view of Isaiah[63] is much easier to subscribe to, when he says that *both* dimensions come from God:

---

[61] Koran, Sura 18, 64-81.
[62] Wilhelm Busch, *Die fromme Helene,* "Schluss."
[63] Isaiah 45, 6-7.

Ego Dominus et non est alter, formans lucem, creans tenebras. Faciens bonum et creans malum: ego Dominus faciens hoc omnia. (I am the Lord, and there is none else. I form the light, and create darkness; I make peace, and create evil; I am the Lord, that doeth all these things.)

In our brief monograph on Asclepios[64] we pointed out that the healing god has dark, chthonic attributes, such as serpent and dog. The healing quality of this wholeness probably explains why the shadow can appear in dreams as a doctor, precisely because he has these healing qualities. The original symbolic unity of light and dark in paganism can be seen most clearly in the 3rd volume of the standard work on Zeus,[65] where over 1000 pages are devoted to his dark side, the Zeus *katach-thonios*.

Resistance to the unconscious in general and to the analytical approach in particular comes as no surprise when we think about the confusing aspects of the shadow. Everything that objects to the rules and regulations of conscious life lurks in the shadow. The shadow creates insubordination, incompetence, lethargy, malice, and unworthiness. It is morally and spiritually inferior and underdeveloped, which is why it often has a "historical" character. The *librium arbitriuni causa peccati* of St. Augustine now takes on a more serious aspect.[66]

In our inferior personality, the inferior function and the opposite attitude obviously lie hidden first and foremost, but they have an effect only as unconscious tendencies and thus also remain autonomous. Unfortunately it also happens that the inferior side becomes independent, and on this basis a neurotic dissociation can set in. This means that the *inferiore* of the conscious personality ought to be connected up, but seeing how this should be done is no easy task. All we can do is acknowledge that these tendencies are part of us, look at them critically, and permit them to surface in a meaningful but moderate way, keeping a happy medium all the while. This cannot come about without a certain amount of insubordination and rebellion, but it can lead to independence, provided the necessary courage also develops to the same extent. As we stated earlier, it is an important moral problem. Unfortunately, however, unless the possibility of desiring to be different exists, ethics have no meaning. In the *Tao Te Ching* of Lao Tse we see what ancient

---

[64] C.A. Meier, *Healing Dream and Ritual*, Daimon, Einsiedeln, 1989.
[65] A.B. Cook, Zeus, Vol. III/I, London 1940.
[66] Augustinus, Confessiones VII/3.

Chinese wisdom has to say on the subject of the genesis of ethics, which is actually expressed in terms of the Jungian tenet of the shadow:

> When the great Tao[67] is lost
> spring forth benevolence and righteousness.
> When wisdom and sagacity arise, there are great hypocrites.
> When family relations are no longer harmonious,
> we have filial children and devoted parents.
> When a nation is in confusion and disorder, patriots are recognized.[68]

Conflicts of duties are an integral part of life and there is no escaping them, unless one prefers to get bogged down in the conflict, thus avoiding any development of consciousness. But this amounts to a dissociation, which also means getting bogged down. Fortunately, this is where dreams may help us because a genuine conflict of conscience always has a mythical character.

Dreams also have a mythical character in that they deal with the creation of consciousness, a sort of microcosmogony. This is why in resolving our conflicts we need a *therapeutic myth*. Also helpful in this respect are such concepts as the fall of man, the virgin birth and Christ's act of redemption. Jung was keen to point out that the new dogma of Pope Pius XII had a healing significance, especially for modern times. In this dogma the Mother of God, her very body – in other words, her material, which is the substratum of all corruption – is carried up into Heaven; the *hyle* is healed, too. If the shadow is largely split off, leading to dissociation, this invariably has strange effects. We need only think of R.L. Stevenson's story of "The Strange Case of Dr. Jekyll and Mr. Hyde" or Heinrich Mann's novel *Prof. Unrat* (which was made into the famous film *Der Blaue Engel*). Such manifestations are fully understood only when one realizes that the shadow is rooted not only in the personal unconscious. Ultimately its roots go much deeper so that the importance of the collective unconscious, the collective shadow, is greater than that of the conscious personality. An example of this greater shadow is Zarathustra in Nietzsche.

His dissociation is described vividly in the poem "Sils Maria":

> Then suddenly, o friend, one became two, and Zarathustra passed me by.[69]

---

[67] Cf. p. 22 ff.
[68] Lao Tse, *Tao Te Ching*, 18, trans. by Ch'u Ta-Kao, 5th edn., London 1959.
[69] trans. D.R.

As is commonly known, Nietzsche's extensive identification with the greater shadow had undesirable effects. For these reasons, shadow figures in dreams must never simply be interpreted *in globo* as belonging to the personality, not even when it transpires that the characteristics represented by them were left in the shadow *per nefas* and could actually be evaluated in positive terms. In both cases, the naively adopting these characteristics could lead to negative or positive inflation, to illusions of grandeur or to a persecution complex. Shadows are forces; we share in them but never completely dominate them.

We would now like to mention just a few of the famous literary works that deal with the shadow problem in its many aspects. The oldest example is undoubtedly the Gilgamesh epic, which came down to us in twelve tablets found in Nineveh in the 19th century as part of the library of the palace of Assurbanipal (4th century B.C.).[70] The Gods send the hero Gilgamesh a *paredros* (friend and companion), the half-bestial Enkidu, who represents the personal shadow of Gilgamesh. They fight and are reconciled, and after that Gilgamesh knows he can count on him (shadow that has become positive). But then the Gods send the giant Humbaba and the bull, who correspond to the collective aspect of the shadow; one might say they represent collective evil, which must simply tale quale be conquered by the hero, i.e., cannot be assimilated.

In Shakespeare, the clearest example of the theme of the "hostile brothers" is probably that of Othello and Iago, and in Goethe it is certainly Faust and Mephistopheles. A very vivid example of what can happen if we allow ourselves to be "taken over" by the shadow can be found in E.T.A. Hoffmann's Brother Medardus in *Die Elixiere des Teufels* (1814). In Carl Spitteler's early work *Prometheus and Epimetheus, a Parable* (1881), Prometheus, as an introvert, clearly represents the soul and Epimetheus, as an extrovert, represents the world. The "ugliest person" in Nietzsche's *Zarathustra* is certainly a classic example of the unreflected shadow.

Generally speaking, hero myths can be understood in terms of the aforementioned "therapeutic myths" in that they show the overcoming of the opposite member, as a result of which the ego grows into the universally human.

---

[70] The text can be found in Alexander Heidel's *The Gilgamesh Epic and Old Testament Parallels*, Chicago, 1946.

Persona

The shadow has been dealt with at some length because its conscious processing is the "be all and end all" of the conflict with the unconscious. The shadow also crucially affects further development in the process of individuation. One must keep in mind, however, that we can never actually complete the task of processing the shadow; it remains something we must work on all our lives. The shadow as part of the collective unconscious is something that cannot be analyzed away or swept under the carpet.

There is also a certain "didactic" reason for our stressing the shadow problem. This is the fact that in the Jungian world there is a tendency in discussions and literature to rush into instances of the unconscious that come up later – such as the anima, animus, Great Mother, Wise Old Man, the Self, and so on – thus glossing over the thorny problem of the shadow. We have shown that any effort to do this is doomed to failure, because there is no way to kill the shadow. In such circumstances the shadow moves into projection and into the collective – the group – manifesting itself in quarrels, divisions and schism. It can easily lead to inflation of the individual, who then sees himself as particularly original and revolutionary, or even believes he has found final solutions to the problems of mankind. This is sufficient reason for our dwelling at length on this subject and less on the typical figures and motifs of the unconscious that usually arise regularly in the further development of the personality. The shorter treatment of these motifs, however, should not detract from their outstanding importance.

In the expression *persona,* Jung is talking more about specific dream *motifs* than about dream *figures.* Thus it often occurs that in our dreams we are naked or there is something embarrassingly wrong about our clothes. Our clothes are part of us and express our special relationship or adaptation to our surroundings. The psychic function corresponding to this relationship is called the persona. As the saying goes, the tailor makes the man, or, to put it more precisely, makes his appearance. Clothes indicate the role we are prepared to play. This is where Jung gets the term "persona," for in ancient theater it was the term used for the stylized *mask* of the actor. *Personam gerere, tenere or ferre* thus means the role that we play or perform in the world. Metaphorically, the expression stands for one's rank: *abest a persona principis or personis summorum virorum non dignum.* Etymologically, the verb *per-sono* = penetrate (through the mask).

Costumes (cf. customs) are indicative of a definite habitual function complex, which is fixed. This is also the case with the persona, which is shaped primarily by one's milieu. One has to "keep face (mask)" and cannot afford to lose it. As our relationship function to the outside world, the persona has two components: the ego and the world. They come into being through the experience of our effect on our surroundings and through the effects of our surroundings on us.

Schopenhauer described this function very clearly as "what one appears to oneself and one's surroundings or in the reflection of one's surroundings;" he went on to warn about "the difference between what one is and what one performs." If someone identifies with this role, he should be discriminated against as "personal." His opposite number would be an "individual" person. The expression "personalities" is based on the same phenomenon and is understood as an unpleasant opposite of perfect adaptation, i.e., as egocentricity, or identification with the persona.

Closer observation reveals that a person with a pronounced persona is all the more susceptible to influences from within. In a vicious circle, this forces him to become increasingly ruthless, more unrelated to and distant from the outside. That such a person is so easily influenced by inner emotions tells us something about the position of the persona in the whole system: as the adaptation system to the outside world, it has a correlative, symmetrical relationship to the adaptation function of the inner world – the anima or the animus.

In terms of the vicious circle, the persona becomes more rigid the more one identifies with it, which makes it not only brittle but also fragile. Cracks start to form, through which the soft center can be seen. Such a person is then suddenly weak, ambivalent and, if he is an intellectual, sentimental, for, as we have said, the anima starts to peep through. Rationalists here show superstitious traits, as can be seen in an experience of *Niels Bohr's,* which he told with great relish: he was calling on an American colleague at his home. Above the house door he noticed a horseshoe. When the professor opened the door, Bohr asked him whether he really believed in nonsense like that. "Of course not," came the answer, "but I have been told that it works even if one doesn't believe in it." This shows us that the rationalist is more superstitious than the superstitious person himself, who always has his doubts, and this is due to penetrating compensatory contributions from the unconscious, which cannot be corrected.

The fate of the persona can be shaped in two different ways:

1. So long as someone is unaware of his persona, it will appear to him in the projection, as always in such a case. Naturally this occurs with people of the same sex. For example, it will be found in the son in a father transference, and with a daughter in a mother transference.
2. The second way of remaining unconscious of one's persona is through identification with it. The commonest form of identification with the role is with the profession or office one holds, the position of dignity that is proudly held as if it were a cross to bear, the special talent of a tenor or a prima donna, or the rank of officer, which was the basis of many jokes in Old Germany.[71] Such people are known to be "personal," sensitive and vehement, which can be seen from the fact that they have a compensatory identity with the anima on the unconscious side. If it comes about in these cases that this anima itself is projected onto a person of the opposite sex, then this gives rise to a compulsory love or love-hate feeling. In this way, even the most ruthless businessman can become totally infatuated with a woman.

To a certain extent we are actually forced to play such roles. In the relevant situation, we have to be the man of the world, the doctor, the professor, the careerist, the priest, and so on. In this respect it is easier for the priest, with his vestments, for he is his clothes. The minute we don a costume (even if it is only a certain hairstyle), this means that we are at least partially aware of it; that is, we do not identify completely. To steer clear of this identification, it is both necessary and psychologically healthy for people in positions of great responsibility to turn this persona into a sort of ritual. Thus, for example, the count who ascends to the throne changes his name, which must be a traditional one. But the *"l'état c'est moi"* of Louis XIV indicates identification. With Ludwig II of Bavaria, however, it proved to be really dangerous, for he identified totally with Louis XIV. This danger existed only, of course, for

---

[71] Cf. G. Meyrink, "Die schwarze Kugel," in *Des deutschen Spiessers Wunderhorn*, Vol. 3, Munich 1913.

absolute monarchs; the "persona" of the king was discussed at great
length by the Renaissance jurists.[72]

Let us turn once again to the words of Lao Tse:

> The great rulers – the people do not notice their existence.
> The lesser ones – they attach to and praise them.
> The still lesser ones – they fear them.
> The still lesser ones – they despise them.
> For when faith is lacking,
> It cannot be met by faith.
> Now how much importance must be attributed to words
> Then when the work is done and things are accomplished,
> People will say that things happened by themselves.
>
> Tao is ever inactive
> And yet there is nothing that it does not do.
> If princes and kings could keep to it,
> All things would of themselves become developed.
> When they are developed, desire would stir in them,
> I would restrain them by the nameless simplicity,
> In order to make them free from desire.
> Free from desire, they would be at rest;
> And the world would of itself become rectified.
>
> Therefore the Sage says:
> Inasmuch as I betake myself to nonaction,
>   the people of themselves become developed.
> Inasmuch as I love quietude,
>   the people of themselves become righteous.
> Inasmuch as I make no fuss,
>   the people of themselves become wealthy.
> Inasmuch as I am free from desire,
>   the people of themselves remain simple.[73]

Generally speaking, it can be said that in women the persona is less
rigid than in men and is therefore more adaptable, just as women change
their clothes and hairstyle more than men do, according to prevailing
fashions. If the persona crops up personified in a dream, then of course
the figure must be of the same sex as the dreamer (as with the shadow).

[72] Cf. Ernst H. Kantorowicz, *The King's Two Bodies, A Study in Medieval Political Theology*, Princeton N.J. 1957.
[73] Lao Tse, *Tao Te Ching*, II, 37 and 57, see fn 68 , p. 89.

Initially there are frequent dreams of the father or the mother. The persona is almost always anthropomorphous and it rarely happens that a "large animal" appears. Here is an example of the dream of a young man in analysis:

> I see myself being carried out in a coffin. It doesn't move me particularly but I *regret very much* being dressed in the coffin in my best and most expensive blue suit if this is what is going to happen to it.

The dreamer, although very young, wants an immaculate persona, which is why he comes over as very impersonal, behaves correctly and will scarcely permit himself a mimical reaction (rigidity of the mask).

As is the case with the shadow, to find out about one's persona one should consult one's opposite sex, i.e., the man, the woman, and the woman the man. A healthy persona development must naturally adapt itself to the phase of life one is going through. For example, a man who is very masculine and an imposing figure, which is right and proper for the first half of life, may find it beneficial in the second half to become gentler.

Anima

As mentioned in the section on the persona, the anima is a function complex that is correlative to the persona, because it represents the function of relation between the ego and the inner world. Anima is one of those expressions characteristic of Jungian psychology, for although it denotes a fundamental dimension, this dimension is by no means elementary but is considerably complex (cf. the term "complex psychology," from the Latin *complector* = "embrace, encompass"). The Latin substantive *anima* (f) originally means breath, "breath of air, wind, air as an element," and also breath in the sense of "breath of life" (*animam finire*) and "soul" as that which animates and stimulates. But the shadows of the underworld are also termed *animae*.

Jung introduced the term anima to denote images stemming from man's unconscious that can be understood as the expression of his soul image. The unconscious counterpart to a man is a woman, the unknown, unconscious "other" in him – a person but not a man. In the process of becoming conscious, especially in the second half of life, images of this kind tend to crop up more frequently with a man and there is plenty of evidence of the universality of this phenomenon. This is why we can go along with Jung and say that it is an archetypal image.

Let us take this opportunity to elaborate on what the term archetype means. With St. Augustine the idea itself in his theory of ideas is an archetypon. He speaks of ideas *"quae ipsae formatae non sunt; quae in divina intelligentia continentur"* (which are not themselves represented forms, but are contained within the mind of God), which is obviously a Platonic idea. But the term goes back further than that and is used by Cicero, as well as Philo of Alexandria[74] and Dionysus of Halikarnassos. It crops up again in the *Anthologia Planudea* and later in the third century in the *Corpus Hermeticum* as "archetypon eidos," corresponding exactly to the archetypal image. Jung came across the same concept once again in Jacob Burckhardt in his letter to A. Brenner, where he talks of "urtümlichen Bildern."[75] Later, to give more emphasis to their functional character, Jung also speaks of such images as "Dominants of the Collective Unconscious." Such dominants are found as common denominators in dreams, visions, hallucinations, but also as mythological motifs of a prototypical nature, which then act as models or patterns for courses of action, making them typical and hence archetypal.

Syzygy is the archetypal motif that corresponds to the fact that within every man is a feminine counterpart. The term "anima" is very complex and we would like to make it easier to understand by listing examples from the histories of religion and culture from different spheres. In so doing, we hope that readers less well-versed in psychology will be able to see that syzygy is as universal as man and woman, although it can be said of it that "The act is common, the perception's not."[76] Syzygy literally means "yoking together," the paired ones, the united ones; the Latin equivalent is "coniunctio" or conjunction, usually represented as the male/female divine couple.

In Vol. 3 of this textbook series, we dealt with Tantra Yoga (Chapter IV), albeit in a different context. Its basis is the syzygy motif of Shiva and Shakti, whose union leads to Brahman. In this volume (Chapter I) we referred to the even more abstract Taoist ideal of equilibrium, i.e., the harmonious union of yang and yin, which corresponds to the Tao. In the Christian religion we should like to remind the reader of Christ

---

[74] Philo of Alexandria, de opifico mundi 71.
[75] Quoted by C.G. Jung in Symbols of Transformation, CW 5, p. 32, fn 45.
[76] Goethe, *Faust*, Prelude on the Stage.

and his bridal church. There is the Gnostic idea of Nous and Sophia. In alchemy there is *sol* and *luna* or *rex* and *regina*. Jung dwells on this subject in "The Psychology of the Transference,"[77] where he uses a very impressive alchemistic woodcut sequence (*Rosarium philosophorum* 1550). Winthuis[78] has much evidence to show that the motif is common among so-called primitives, but we find he goes too far in his theories. We shall give some examples relevant for Western man.

The oldest illustration of the syzygy motif is probably that found in Empedocles. He taught that the *sphairos* was the condition of the universe which, through the action of love and strife, is eternally constructed, destroyed and constructed anew.

> There the swift limbs of the sun are not distinguished, nor the shaggy might of earth, nor sea. In this way it is held fast in the close covering of harmony, a rounded sphere, rejoicing in encircling stillness.
>
> No discord or unseemly warring in the limbs.
>
> But he is equal to himself in every direction, without any beginning or end, a rounded sphere, rejoicing in encircling stillness.
>
> For two branches do not spring from his back, he has no feet, no swift knees, no organs of reproduction, but he is equal to himself in every direction, a rounded sphere.
>
> They are as they were before (Love and Strife) and shall be, and never, I think, will endless time be emptied of these two.
>
> A twofold tale I shall tell: at one time it grew to be one only from many, and at another again it divided to be many from one. There is a double birth of what is mortal, and a double passing away; for the uniting of all things brings one generation into being and destroys it, and the other is reared and scattered as they are again being divided. And these things never cease their continual exchange of position, at one time all coming together into one through love, at another again being borne away from each other by strife's repulsion. (So, insofar as one is accustomed to arise from many) and many are produced from one as it is again being divided, to this extent they are born and have no abiding life; but insofar as they never cease their continual exchange, so far they are forever unaltered in the cycle.
>
> But come, hear my words, for learning brings an increase of wisdom. Even as I said before, when I was stating the range of my discourse, a twofold tale I shall tell: at one time it grew to be one only from many, and

[77] C.G. Jung, Psychology of the Transference, CW 16, German original 1946.
[78] J. Winthuis, *Das Zweigeschlechterwesen bei den Zentralaustraliern und anderen Völkern* (The Double-Gendered Being Among the Peoples of Central Australia and Others), Leipzig, 1928.

at another again it divided to be many from one – fire and water and earth and measureless height of air, with pernicious strife apart from these, matched (to them) in every direction, and love among them, their equal in length and breadth. Contemplate her with the mind, and do not sit staring dazed; she is acknowledged to be inborn also in the bodies of men, and because of her, their thoughts are friendly and they work together, giving her the name Joy, as well as Aphrodite. No mortal has perceived her as she whirls among them."[79]

In the *Symposium,* Plato has a no less interesting myth. After Aristophanes has celebrated Eros as the greatest doctor, he goes on to explain syzygy's origins as follows:

And first let me treat of the nature and the state of man, for the original human nature was not like the present, but different. In the first place, the sexes were originally three in number, not two as they are now; there was man, woman, and the union of the two, having a name corresponding to this double nature (which was once called Androgynous); this once had a real existence, but is now lost, and the name only is preserved as a term of reproach. In the second place, the primeval man was round and had four hands and four feet, back and sides forming a circle, one head with two faces, looking opposite ways, set on a round neck and precisely alike; also four ears, two privy members, and the remainder to correspond. When he had a mind he could walk as men now do, and he could also roll over and over at a great rate, leaning on his four hands and four feet, eight in all, like tumblers going over and over with their legs in the air; this was when he wanted to run fast. Now there were these flee sexes, because the sun, moon, and earth are three; and the man was originally the child of the sun, the woman of the earth, and the man-woman of the moon, which is made up of sun and earth, and they were all round and moved round and round like their parents. Terrible was their might and strength, and the thoughts of their hearts were great, and they made an attack upon the gods; and of them is told the tale of Otus and Ephialtes who, as Homer says, dared to scale heaven, and would have laid hands upon the gods. Doubt reigned in the councils of Zeus and of the gods. Should they kill them and annihilate the race with thunderbolts, as they had done the giants, then there would be an end of the sacrifice and worship which men offered to them; but, on the other hand, the gods could not suffer their insolence to be unrestrained. At last, after a good deal of reflection, Zeus discovered a way. He said: "I have a notion which will humble their pride and mend their manners; they shall continue to exist, but I will cut them in two and then they will be diminished in strength and

[79] Empedocles, fr. 27-29 and 16-17.

increased in numbers; this will have the advantage of making them more profitable to us. They shall walk upright on two legs, and if they continue insolent and won't be quiet, I will split them again and they shall hop about on a single leg." He spoke and cut them in two, like a sorb-apple which is halved for pickling, or as you might divide an egg with a hair; and as he cut them one after another, he bade Apollo give the face and the half of the neck a turn in order that the man might contemplate the section of himself: this would teach him a lesson of humility. He was also to heal their wounds and compose their forms. Apollo twisted the face and pulled the skin all around over that which in our language is called the belly, like the purses which draw in, and he made one mouth at the centre, which he fastened in a knot (this is called the navel); he also moulded the breast and took out most of the wrinkles, much as a shoemaker might smooth out leather upon a last; he left a few, however, in the region of the belly and navel, as a memorial of the primeval change. After the division the two parts of man, each desiring his other half, came together, and threw their arms about one another eager to grow into one....

Suppose Hephaestus, with his instruments, were to come to the pair who are lying side by side and say to them, "What do you people want of one another?" They would be unable to explain. Suppose further, that when he saw their perplexity he said: "Do you desire to be wholly one; always day and night to be in one another's company? For if this is what you desire, I am ready to melt you into one and let you grow together, so that being two you shall become one, and while you live, live a common life as if you were a single man, and after your death in the world below still be one departed soul instead of two – I ask whether this is what you lovingly desire, and whether you are satisfied to attain this?" There is not a man among them when he heard this who would deny or who would not acknowledge that this meeting and melting in one another's arms, this becoming one instead of two, was the very expression of his ancient need. And the reason is that human nature was originally one and we were a whole, and the desire and pursuit of the whole is called love.[80]

Of course, not all the participants in the Symposium are convinced this is the genesis of Eros, and we have introduced the myth just as an illustration to show how widespread the syzygy motif is. It convinces us that in every man there is a "woman" and in every woman there is a "man." As this countersexual content is latent, i.e., initially appears only in the form of unconscious images, we can truly say that "the act is common, the perception's not."

[80] Plato, Symposium, 189 d 1 ff. and 192e.

These days men tend to formulate the question as to the sources of the syzygy motif and hence the anima (and for women the animus) somewhat differently, and thus probably discover several roots. The first thing to consider is the man's real woman or wife and the woman's real man or husband, and here the roots are found on the level of the sensual domain. Second, the sum of all the man's experiences with women, and vice-versa, also play a role, starting with the mother and father, sisters and brothers. This is actually the psychic equivalent of the first point. Third, as the myths have just proven, we must assume that in the unconscious of every man is an archetypal image of woman, and of every woman, an archetypal image of man. Whether or not the so-called "countersexual genes," if they exist, should be taken into consideration is a question that probably cannot be settled on a scientific basis, and is therefore "senseless" in the pragmatic sense of the term.

Generally speaking, we can say that the existence of countless divine couples in the history of religion is the basis of our hypothesis, and that the syzygy is thus a *theistic* idea. This indisputable fact proves that behind it is not just the human couple, as Freud says, but the projection of unknown contents, because only contents of the unconscious can be projected, whereas the real parental couple is certainly very well-known to us. Moreover, in many cultures there is still the tradition of choosing a second parental couple when a child is born and in English they are in fact known as the godfather and godmother, terms which once again indicate the importance of the presence of a "divine" couple. The godparents stand behind the parents just as the gods stand behind the divine images.

A variant of syzygy is the image of an androgynous god, in which the two components appear as a bisexual entity rather than as a couple. The "eternal embrace" has here become a melting into one. We shall ignore the fact here that in certain circumstances we must take into account a differentiation that has not yet come about, as is the case, for example, in India in the Brhadaranyaka Upanishad (approx. 9th-8th century B.C.) (1.4,3). There it says:

> Verily, he had no delight. Therefore one alone has no delight. He desired a second. He was, indeed, as large as a woman and a man closely embraced. He caused that self to fall into two pieces. Therefrom arose a husband and a wife. Therefore this is true: "Oneself is like a half-fragment" as Yajnavalkya used to say. Therefore this space is filled by a wife. He copulated with her. Therefrom human beings were produced."[81]

[81] R.E. Hume, *The Thirteen Principal Upanishads*, London 1931, p. 81.

Examples in which the divine figure sometimes appears in masculine form, sometimes in feminine, often occur in the visions of religious people. Let us take a look at what the Swiss saint Bruder Klaus has to say.[82] This is his third vision:

A man interrupted his sleep because of God and his suffering and he gave thanks to God for his suffering and torment. And God showed him mercy, so that he found pleasure in it. Whereupon he lay down to rest. And when his reason was bound up in chains and yet he felt he had not fallen asleep, it seemed to him as if someone had come through the door, was standing in the middle of the house, asking him in a powerful, clear voice what his name was and then saying: "Come and see your father and watch what he is doing!"

And it seemed to him that he soon covered the distance traveled by an arrow and arrived at a beautiful tent in a spacious hall. There he saw that there were people living in it, and with him was the one who had called him, standing by his side and speaking on his behalf like a spokesman. And although he was speaking, he could not see the figure, nor was he curious about it, and he spoke on his behalf, saying: "This is the one who picked up your son and carried him and came to his aid in his fear and need. Thank him and be grateful." There came a handsome majestic man through the palace, with a shining color in his face, and in a white garment, like a priest in his vestment. And he laid both arms on his shoulders and pressed him close and thanked him with all the fervent love of his heart, because he had stood by his son and helped him in his need. And the man was taken aback and afraid, declaring himself to be unworthy and saying: "I do not know whether I have ever been of service to your son." At this the figure departed and was not seen again.

And then there came a beautiful majestic woman through the palace, also in a white garment. And he could see that the white garment was newly washed. And she laid both arms on his shoulders and pressed him close to her with an overflowing love, because he had stood so faithfully by her son in his need. And the man was afraid and said: "I do not know whether I have ever been of service to your son, except that I came here to see what you were doing." Then she departed and he saw her no more.[83]

He then looked around him. And he saw the son sitting in a chair, also wearing a similar garment; it was spotted with red as if someone had splashed it with a frond. And the son bowed his head to him and thanked

[82] In P. Alban Stoeckli, *Die Visionen des seligen Bruder Klaus*, Einsiedeln 1933, p. 20.
[83] trans. D.R.

him deeply for helping him in his need. When the man looked down he saw that he, too, was wearing a white garment spattered with red, like the son. He was astonished for he had not realized that he was wearing it. Soon afterwards he found himself back at the place where he had lain down, so that he did not think he had been asleep. Amen."[84]

Here God is seen once as the Royal Father and once as the Royal Mother. To show that there is nothing unique or unusual about this Swiss vision from the 15th century, we should like to produce a similar example from a different time and culture. This is a vision of Anna Kingsford's. She was the founder of the "Hermetic Society" and the "Esoteric Christian Union," a vegetarian and an anti-vivisectionist, who lived in England at the end of the 19th century. The text of the vision is:

> It was God as the Lord who by his duality proves that God is substance as well as power, love as well as will, feminine as well a masculine, mother as well as father.[85]

It should be noted that the first vision is from a man and the second from a woman, as is Mary Baker Eddy's odd amendment to the beginning of the Lord's Prayer: "Our Father-Mother God."[86]

If we draw psychological consequences from these different examples, they may be summed up as follows: In every masculine being something feminine is given, and vice versa. In the case of the man, for example, we would also say that his masculine (conscious) side compensates itself by this inner, feminine (unconscious) image. As woman is to man the most unknown of all beings, this anima image can only represent his unconscious; that is, it is the exponent or representative of his unconscious. It is in this sense that we have to understand Jung's term *anima*.

It was because these fundamental images and psychic laws were so common that Jung coined the phrase "archetypal images." The archetype behind these images would consequently be in an a *priori* state of readiness to shape apperception in a specific way. This would be a formal condition. When we phrase it like that, we are getting pretty close to *instinct,* but this is not the place to go into such a complicated

[84] Cf. also C.G. Jung, "Bruder Klaus," Neue Schweizer Rundschau I/4, Zürich 1933, pp. 223-229. Now in CW 11, p. 316.
[85] Edward Maitland, *Anna Kingsford, Her Life, Letters, Diary and Work*, 2 vols., London 1896, I, p. 129f.
[86] Mary Baker Eddy, *Science and Health*, 16. 1875.

matter. The reader will find most of the arguments concerning instinct and archetype clearly compiled in H. Heusser's (ed.) *"Instinkte und Archetypen im Verhalten der Tiere und im Erleben des Menschen"* (*Wege der Forschung,* Vol. 80), Darmstadt 1976. Jung dwelt at length on the subject in his 1946 Eranos lecture.[87] What we wish to make clear is that the archetype represents all our inherent *possibilities* for ideas and concepts (not hereditary ones, of course). We are inevitably reminded that this statement also applies to the "subjective factor" of the introvert, and to the "numinal accent" (cf. Chapter III above and Vol. 3 of this textbook series). Behind these two dimensions, too, there is ultimately an archetype.

As the being of the opposite sex (the anima in man and the animus in woman) is unconscious, it always appears in projected form. Thus the anima is the projection-producing factor *par excellence* in a man. The most impressive and probably the most complete description of this is given in the Indian fantasy of the Maya, the spinner and illusion-creating dancer. Indian phenomenology can easily be read today in Heinrich Zimmer,[88] and also in Arwind Vasavada.[89] Clearly, the complex wealth of the unconscious images a man is capable of projecting onto a woman (and vice versa) is responsible for many of the beautiful and sad things that happen to us in life. "Pleasure or pain to one another living!"[90]

What Jung is trying to get at with the expression *anima* can perhaps be best defined through a process of elimination, when one says that the anima is what remains when the real woman is taken away from the man's image of her. Because the anima image is initially in the unconscious, it has a chance to appear only in dreams and fantasies. The corresponding personifications, however, in addition to the familiar characteristics of a specific woman, also have features that are odd, alien and numinous. Archaic, or at least historical, characteristics also crop up, corresponding to the archaic qualities of the unconscious.

Anima figures usually start to appear frequently in dreams only in the second half of life, because in the first half they remain in the lap of the

---

[87] C.G. Jung, Der Geist der Psychologie, *Eranos-Jahrbuch 1946* (XXIV), Zürich 1947, pp. 385-490. CW 8, 2. ed. Olten 1977, *Die Dynamik des Unbewußten,* pp. 183-261.
[88] Heinrich Zimmer, *Maya, der indische Mythos,* Stuttgart 1936, Chap. I.
[89] A.U. Vasavada, *Tripura Rahasya* (Jnanakanda), Varanasi 1965.
[90] Byron, *The Pilgrimage of Childe Harold,* 1812.

mother complex. In the second half of life, following the transformation discussed above, in which values begin to change their meaning, the development veers away from the mother, and only as death approaches does it return to her "in changed form," i.e., to Mother Earth.

If one attempts to define the anima as a psychic function, then one can say it represents the relation function to the inner world. Jung talks here of a "maternal Eros" and it is important for a man to achieve this relationship in the second half of life.

There are, of course, several common ways of reacting to the inner world. The one that remains predominant today is unwavering self-control. Our feeling is that this is commonly compensated for through insomnia. Equally popular is a sort of emotional lightness and a concomitant ability to express emotions freely. This is more common in southern climes (Latin lover) but also entails a relative feminization – "the woman in the man." This sort of compensatory effect is probably more common in men who are consciously very critical, negative or who, on the other hand, are very optimistic. Let us not forget that as expressions of the unconscious (the anima) these predominantly emotional characteristics are always autonomous. Generally speaking, these primitive anima expressions tend to reinforce everything, to exaggerate, but also to distort. In particular they will mythologize our relationships to people and profession, especially when we are emotionally involved. The web of fantasy that lies behind them, if strongly constellated by the situation, will make the man susceptible, touchy, moody, jealous, vain and unadaptable. In short, it softens him and gives him effeminate reactions. He becomes the strong man with the gentle nature.

It is obvious that given the interaction between the conscious and the unconscious, any active preoccupation with the dream anima figures is bound to affect their phenomenology, and it is in light of this retroactive effect that we are to understand Parmenides when he said in his poetry "and the girls *point the way*."[91] Jung attributes to this development a fundamental role in the process of becoming conscious. He gives five stages of development for the anima image:

1. Initially it must be assumed that the anima will be projected onto the mother as the central feminine figure. This is the source of the so-

[91] Parmenides, fr. 1, 5. Diels / Kranz, *Die Fragmente der Vorsokratiker,* 6th edn., Berlin 1951, I, p. 228.

called mother complex. It is made up of a) the mother as a woman, b) the mother imago and c) the mother image contaminated with the preexisting image of the anima. The mother image is the image of the *subjective relationship* to the mother object. The mother complex itself should and can be dissolved completely, because it is a *complexus delendus*. If this does not happen, it will lead to promiscuity, Don Juanism, homosexuality and even criminality, because in the lap of the all-bountiful "mother" all things are allowed. This has been seen on occasion in the alma maters of the universities. It is in this light that we are to understand the famous sculptor Ernst Barlach in his drama *Der tote Tag* when he has the mother of the son who wishes to become a hero say, "He should bury his mother first."[92]

2. The second stage, beginning at about adolescence, is that of the maid or the substitute mother, the older girlfriend of a young man (cf. the marshall's wife for Octavian in "Rosenkavalier").

3. The third stage Jung calls the prostitute type. It corresponds to a somewhat androgynous woman, and has become very modern with modern sexual liberalization. Its archetypal prototype is "Baubo." She was an autochthon in Eleusis, serving Demeter as a wet nurse. She is said to be the inspirer of the obscene jokes of the women of Athens, which were part of the ritual of transferring the Kephissos along the sacred procession to the Demeter festivals in Eleusis. At one time, Baubo had been able to cheer up the mourning Demeter with an obscene gesture. The ritual even has its own technical terms: γεφύρισμος and αἰσχρολογία, and Iacchus (festival name of the mystic Bacchus of Eleusis) made such an obscene gesture as a child (he was the son of Demeter and Zeus and brother of the Kore). One thinks automatically of the almost ritualistic telling of dirty jokes at a certain age. Let us mention in passing that this is the Iacchus described by Ovid *(Metamorphoses* IV, 18-20) as a *puer aeternus,* eternal boy, and this is where Jung got the term from.

4. The fourth stage is called the priestess type. The figures appearing in the dreams here are beautiful nurses or nuns, or other women with some sort of ineffable holiness.

5. The fifth stage is the so-called *femme inspiratrice.* This figure has a brilliant, witty, clever and cunning quality, but is also mysterious,

[92] Ernst Barlach, *Der tote Tag*, Berlin 1925, p. 31.

enigmatic, taciturn and mystical. Representatives of this type are such *grandes dames* as Ninon de Lenclos.

Clearly, all these images have a demonic effect on the man when projected onto a woman, turning her into *a femme fatale*. There is no doubt that in every case of "love at first sight" it is a case of anima projection, for at "first sight" the woman is obviously largely unknown and for the man is therefore a suitable carrier of the unknown (unconscious) image. Hence the presentient feeling of an old acquaintance.

Let us now take a look at historical and literary evidence of the role and development of the anima. Particularly interesting is the story of Simon Magus, which we know from the *Acts of the Apostles* (8:5-24) and from Irenaus and Hippolytus. Simon's name lived on for centuries in the word *simony,* which was named after him, and reminds us of the delight some people have when cases of bribery are brought to light. Simon lived in Samaria and Rome in the 1st century and was a real rival to Peter, John and Philip. He declared himself the "highest god." He was always accompanied by a lady called Helena, who he said was the divine *ennoia* (notion), the power contained in the *aion* (age), who was also a *charis* (grace) and who made *aion* long for the women, so that *anthropos* was begotten. He claimed that after the emanation out of the *aion* this Helena was imprisoned under demonic force in several women figures, the last being Helena, and had been freed by him, Simon. He had discovered her in a brothel in Tyrus and bought her release. He called her his "first thought" and the "supreme mother." One should not be distracted by the influence of Gnosticism on Simon's terminology but should concentrate rather on the different stages of the anima referred to above. In the Gnostic speculations the mother type is represented by Eve, the whore appears in Helena (of Troy), the saint in Maria and the *femme inspiratrice* type in Sophia.

This automatically makes us think of Goethe's Faust, where a similar development of the feminine element is found. It moves from Gretchen to Helena (heathen, stage 3), from there to Maria (Christian, stage 4), ending up finally with the "eternally feminine" (Sophia, stage 5). In Goethe we also find the enigmatic figure of Mignon who, in *Wilhelm Meister's theatralische Sendung,*[93] takes the masculine article, i.e., has androgynous characteristics (cf. stage 3 above). With Goethe the role of

---

[93] Goethe, *Wilhelm Meisters theatralische Sendung*, Book 3, Chap. 8.

the femme inspiratrice was played especially by Frau von Stein, elo-
quent evidence of which is his poem to her of April 14, 1776, rendered
here in a prose translation:

> *Why did you give us deep insight,* visions and surmisings of our future, so
> that we can never live in trustful abandonment to our love, to our earthly
> happiness, in an illusion of joy? O Fate, why did you give us these
> intuitions, give us each other's heart to contemplate, and make us see
> through all these strange confusions of feelings and discern what we truly
> are to each other?
>
> Oh, there are so many thousands of men and women with scarcely any
> knowledge of their own hearts, drifting insensitively through life, floating
> aimlessly hither and thither, running hopelessly from unforeseen suffering,
> and exulting again at the unexpected daybreak of lively joys. Only we, two
> poor loving souls, are denied the mutual happiness of loving each other
> without understanding each other – of each seeing in the other something
> the other never was, of forever setting out afresh in the pursuit of illusory
> happiness and faltering, too, before illusory dangers.
>
> Happy are those whom an empty dream preoccupies! Happy are they
> whose surmisings would be mere vanity! Our every meeting, alas, and our
> every look, only confirms the truth of our surmise and our dream. Oh tell
> me, what does Fate hold in store for us? Tell me, how did it fashion between
> us so pure and strict a bond? *Oh, in far bygone times you were my sister or
> my wife.*

In this connection, Jung often quoted the novel *She*[94] by Rider
Haggard (1856-1925), as well as the strikingly similar *L'Atlantide*[95] by
Pierre Benoit (1886-1962). In the two works *La prêtresse d'Isis*[96] and
Femmes inspiratrices et poètes annonciateurs (1907),[97] Edouard
Schuré (1841-1929) dealt with both fantasy figures and historical
women who have played the roles of the fifth stage. Probably the most
famous example of this function in the woman is with Cosima Liszt and
Mathilde Wesendonck in *Richard Wagner,* which we spoke about
earlier. And in Spitteler's *Imago,*[98] too, the subject matter is the
"Mistress soul" as *domina severa,* reminding us of "She-who-must-be-
obeyed."

---

[94] Henry Rider Haggard, *She,* London 1887.
[95] Pierre Benoit, *L'Atlantide,* Paris 1918-1919.
[96] Edouard Schuré, *La prêtresse d'Isis,* 4th edn., Paris 1927.
[97] Idem, *Femmes inspiratrices et poètes annonciateurs,* Paris 1907.
[98] Carl Spitteler, *Imago,* Jena 1906. Collected works IV, Zürich (no year given).

A document of great literary merit on the subject of the anima is the autobiographical *Mémoires d'Outre-tombe* (1803-1831) by François René de Chateaubriand (1768-1848). It is rarely quoted, so we shall do so here:

A neighboring landlord from Combourg, accompanied by his pretty wife, had come to spend a few days in our castle. I no longer recall what was happening in the village, but we all ran to the window of the large hall in order to look out. I was the first to reach the window, closely followed by my neighbor's wife. I wanted to make room for her and turned round. Unintentionally she blocked my way and I was pressed between her and the window. I no longer knew what was going on around me. From that moment I realized that in a way that was as yet unknown to me, to love and to be loved must be the ultimate form of happiness. Had I done what other men do, I should soon have discovered the joys and sorrows whose seed I bore within me. But with me everything assumed unusual forms. My burning fantasy, my shyness and the loneliness were such that instead of looking around me I turned in on myself. In the absence of a real object, I created a phantom for myself through the strength of my vague desires, a phantom that stayed with me. I do not know whether the history of the human heart has ever produced a similar case of this kind.

I made one single woman out of all the women I had ever seen. She had the figure, the hair and the smile of the stranger who had pressed me to her bosom, the eyes and the skin of one or other of the girls in the village. Other features were provided by the portraits hanging in the salon of ladies from the time of Franz I, Heinrich IV and Ludwig XIV; I even borrowed from the paintings of the Madonna in churches.

This magic image was my invisible companion wherever I went; I talked to it as if to a real person. Depending on the degree of my mania, the figure turned into Aphrodite without her veil, Diana in pink and azure, Thalia with her comic mask, Hebe with the bowl of youth; the dream figure often turned into a fairy who held Nature in her sway. I continually improved the painting and when I had completed a masterpiece I dissolved the drawing and the colors; out of one woman there were many. I worshipped all the individual charms that I had worshipped as one entity. Pygmalion did not love his statue to this degree. My sole concern was to please mine. Not seeing in myself anything that could evoke love, I extravagantly bestowed on myself all those qualities I lacked. I rode like Castor and Pollux, played the lyre like Apollo, was more powerful and skilled with weapons than Mars himself. Be it with historical heroes or heroes from novels, I amassed concocted adventures on concocted foundations: the shadows of the daughters of Morvin, the wives of the Sultans of Baghdad or Granada, the noble wives of city elders, baths, perfumes, dances, all the pleasures of the Orient, all this was given to me by a magic wand of my own.

On waking from these dreams, when I came to myself, without fame, without beauty, without talent, a poor, little fellow from Brittany whom nobody would so much as glance at, and whom no woman would ever love, I was seized with despair. I no longer dared to look up at the radiant picture that was ever with me. This mania lasted two whole years, during which time the adulating excitation of my soul readied its climax. I spoke little, did not speak at all, cast my books aside. My inclination to loneliness grew apace. I bore all the signs of a violent passion, was hollow-eyed, thin, short of sleep, vacant, sad, unapproachable and violent. These were strange days for me, void of human contact, and without any meaning – and yet they were also days of bliss.[99]

These lines should speak for themselves, without need of commentary. This is equally true of Dante, who, *"nel mezzo del cammin di nostra vita,"*[100] i.e., at the turning point in life and thus at the beginning of his magnum opus, encounters Beatrice, his anima. Somewhat later in the Italian Renaissance we find a most remarkable novel, probably from the pen of a Venetian Dominican monk, Francesco Colonna, with the unusual title *Hypnerotomachia Poliphili.*[101] The work came out in 1499 with Aldus Manutius and is decorated with a number of splendid woodcuts from the Mantegnas school. It is one of the most costly incunabula there is, but we have easy access to it through a French translation with an alchemistic commentary by Béroalde de Verville.[102] There has been an excellent study of the work in more recent times by Linda Fierz-David.[103] The title is a neologism, made up of the three Greek words for sleep, love and battle. In a dream, the author ends up in the Black Forest (Herkynia silva); there he keeps losing his way and encounters many dangers but finally meets the girl Polia. He has always known her and loved her since his youth (eros of distance), which is why he is called Poliphilo. There then follows a sort of courtly love, with the corresponding changes in the anima figure Polia, who had previously been dedicated to the chaste Diana; she is converted to Venus and finally disappears into higher spheres, thus hinting at the

[99] F.R. Chateaubriand, *Mémoires d'Outre-tombe*, Paris 1848.
[100] Dante, *La divina commedia*, Inferno, Canto primo, I.
[101] Franceso Colonna, *Hypnerotomachia Poliphili*, Venice 1499.
[102] *Le songe de Poliphile*, Payot, Paris 1926.
[103] Linda Fierz-David, *The Dream of Poliphilo*. Spring, Dallas, 1987.

subject of the death marriage. In French archaeology there is an expression for this: *"eros funéraire."*

The sequence of stages in anima development given above (based on Jung) show that over the years a transformation from initially dark figures emerges into lighter ones. In dreams it is almost always an unknown woman, and the initially dark anima aspect manifests itself in the fact that the woman may be of dubious or even repulsive character, a sick woman or a *"femme qui se fait suivre."* She is frequently foreign or primitive, in white men, for example, a black girl, in non-Jewish men a Jewish girl. These figures are often behind the times in their appearance; i.e., they may have historical features, or may even be out of time altogether. Another common feature is the phenomenon Freud referred to as compression, meaning that they are composite figures, uniting the qualities of mother, sister, wife and daughter. One is reminded of Doctor Marianus at the end of *Faust* II:

> Virgin, Mother, Queen,
> Goddess, be gracious!

If the anima presents itself in theriomorphic form in dreams, it is usually as an animal of prey or a snake.

Typical carriers of projections are especially women of striking appearance, of whom there is no shortage in advanced civilizations. Very dark or very blonde or red hair seems to be particularly appropriate. There is a preference for dancers and actresses. But women with totally expressionless faces also lend themselves to projections of all kinds.

These characteristics, brought up by the anima, now have to be integrated on the psychological level; i.e., they must be made conscious. Let us once again stress that what this means is that the *effects and the contents* must be led to consciousness, for only these can be made conscious. The anima itself as an archetype is a consciousness-transcending factor beyond the influence of perception and arbitrariness: the unconscious is really unconscious, as Jung so concisely stated, and fortunately it can be neither fathomed (Heraclitus) nor exhausted. But integration with these anima qualities produces an eros of consciousness in a man – a maternal eros of the mature man – giving the masculine consciousness the quality of relatedness, a gain that cannot be overestimated.

The subject of the anima is inexhaustible in life, for life goes on, continually producing further manifestations and movements of this dominant factor of the unconscious. There is, however, one condition if coming to terms with the anima is to have a successful outcome: the shadow and the persona must be adequately integrated beforehand. This is a prerequisite for a person's relationship with members of his or her own sex, whereas the integration of the anima affects a man's relationship with members of the opposite sex and the world in general. Looking back on our observations concerning typology, we see that with the shadow and the anima we are in the sphere of the inferior function, so it is clear that the objective is extremely difficult to attain.

To conclude, here is one further theoretical consequence of what has just been said: the integration of the element of the opposite sex produces a triad, consisting of

1. The male subject,
2. The female object (in the partner, in a real woman),
3. The anima, as a third element, which is transcendent.

In the course of the individuation process a fourth figure begins to appear, the figure of what Jung termed

4. The "archetype of the wise old man."

We have a highly authentic record of this in *Memories, Dreams, Reflections by C.G. Jung*, ed. A. Jaffé, Zürich, 1962, trans. by Richard and Clara Winston, New York and London, 1963.

Animus

When discussing the animus, the same prerequisites apply as for the anima. This is particularly true of its origins in syzygy, and so it is essential for the reader to have digested the comments on the syzygy motif in the previous section. The conclusions arrived at there can simply be reversed when dealing with a feminine system: in a woman's system there must also be a masculine element – hence the Latin masculine *animus*. Initially it means "soul, spirit," and in relation to thinking it means "spirit, thought, reason." *Meo animo* means, for example, "in my opinion, my thinking." Jung uses the noun more in the sense of spirit than of opinion, tenet, principle.

Like the anima in man, the animus comes to the fore in the second half of life. With the woman, however, the hormonal component is more pronounced; she starts to grow a moustache, for example, her voice gets deeper and she becomes more energetic.

Although the animus in the woman's system has the same position as the anima in man, what may be surprising to learn that its phenomenology is very different from that of the anima. *La petite différence anatomique* is considerably greater in the psychological sphere. In so far as the animus must be regarded as the legitimate function complex of the woman, the whole universal difference between man and woman could be discussed from this angle. It would then emerge that the modern egalitarianism of man and woman (women's liberation, etc.) is a fatal error, for it is precisely this difference between the sexes, especially the psychological one, that makes life interesting and keeps the ball rolling, as the saying goes. There is no denying that it can make life complicated, but we merely wish to point out that a deeper knowledge of the real differences between the two is likely to be more productive than a declaration of war.

The legacy of Jung, and especially Emma Jung,[104] could be a starting point for a reconciliation, but unfortunately this is too irksome a process for belligerent animi, and unassuming heroism is not their style. At this point we must not fail to refer to the original representation of the development of the animus, as depicted by Toni Wolff,[105] for she has given a most impressive typology of the feminine psyche.

It seems, however, that in the West at least, cultural development has not offered the animus sufficient opportunity to pursue a natural course. As with the anima, a conscious coming to terms with the animus ought to provide a basis for any creative achievement, in that it leads to harmonious integration, a synthesis of the masculine and the feminine, enabling it to bear fruit. This is why, only recently, creative women have become more common.

However, as the animus usually fancies it has to assert itself as a spiritual principle against the man, although this is not a conscious

---

[104] Emma Jung, *Animus and Anima*, New York 1957.
[105] Cf. Toni Wolff, *Studien zu C.G. Jungs Psychologie*, Zürich 1981, p. 257 ff and p. 269 ff.

intention, it manifests itself in a form that is bound to be objectionable to the man. Such animus effects, for example, are niggling and splitting hairs, arguing about principles and ideas, being dogmatic. She begins to be a know-all and clings obsessively to her ideas. An animus obsession, i.e., lengthy spells when this unconscious factor dominates, often leads to religious sectarianism or tenacious adherence to some trendy philosophy.

Analytical experience has shown that conscious processing of the animus can be brought about better between two women (analyst and analysand), which may be because in such a situation the "battle of the sexes" is not a factor and it is thus possible to work on a more objective basis.

Jung asserted that there were three stages in the development of the animus. The first stage is that of the *father complex*. A girl is attracted to older men; they can be paternal friends or teachers. The second stage is what Jung calls the *stage of action*. The representatives of this stage are usually "hero types," such as prizefighters, pilots, tanned sportsmen, preferably blue-eyed, and tenors. In the negative case, they may be criminals, albeit physically attractive ones. Jung called the third stage the *spiritual stage*. It manifests itself mainly in projections onto parsons, teachers, doctors, actors and artists. Negatively, there can be swindlers, impostors, misunderstood geniuses or big talkers.

During these stages of development, the figures of the second stage may appear in dreams as pilots, racing drivers, chauffeurs, hairdressers, and in the third stage as priests, sorcerers or very old men. Theriomorphically, the commonest figures are birds, especially eagles. When the animus has reached a high potential and at the same time is projected onto a real man, this can lead to anything between sexual bondage and spiritual servitude.

The scientific processing of the manifestations of the animus is still in the early stages. The first and as yet the best contribution on the subject comes from Emma Jung, with the essay "Ein Beitrag zum Problem des Animus."[106] Esther Harding deals with the history of the development of the animus in *The Way of All Women*.[107] There is a wealth of illustrative material in the so-called "controls" of female mediums in spiritualism, which are always masculine. A remarkable

[106] Emma Jung, *Animus and Anima*, Dallas (various editions).
[107] Esther Harding, *The Way of All Women*, New York 1933.

example of this is the representation of the case of Mlle Smith with her "control," who calls himself Leopold, in Th. Flournoy.[108] As examples from literature, Jung often refers to Ronald Fraser's tale of *The Flying Draper*[109] and especially the novel by H.G. Wells (1866-1946) *Christina Alberta's Father,*[110] which is a veritable treasure trove for complex manifestations of all kinds.

In H.G. Wells we can see a peculiarity of the animus that we have not yet mentioned: for Christina Alberta the animus is represented in the form of a "court of conscience," i.e., a tribunal made up of *several* men. This plurality is actually a characteristic of the animus, so that one is tempted to replace the term animus by the plural animi. The anima, by way of contrast, is usually just one woman, and although it has dark and light aspects, this ambivalence can be found in one and the same personification. Jung occasionally tried to clarify this difference between the animus and the anima by pointing out the compensatory function of these elements in relation to the conscious. Masculine consciousness is known to have a polygamous tendency, to which the unconscious, with the single anima figure, reacts monogamously. Feminine consciousness, however, is monogamously orientated, with the polygamous tendency being confined to the unconscious, and hence the animus can be perceived in plurality.

Once the shadow and the persona have been integrated, the woman's next objective in the process of personality development is the integration of the animus. We must repeat that it is not possible to make conscious the archetype of the animus. What can be integrated are its effects, which must each be clearly distinguished, so that they are no longer autonomous, for here we come close to the "discrimination of the spirits" in I Cor. 12:10.[111] On the other hand, there has to be a relationship to the images and the effects, for only then is it possible to have some sort of check with a certain amount of "mutual respect." In this way, the animus gradually develops into a *logos,* which gives the feminine consciousness a sort of reflectiveness, meditativeness and perceptiveness; in other words, it will acquire new characteristics, the effects of which will be particularly beneficial in relation to the partner.

[108] Th. Flournoy, *Des Indes à la planète Mars*, Paris/Geneva 1900.
[109] R. Fraser, *The Flying Draper*, London 1924 (The Traveller's Library, London 1931).
[110] H.G. Wells, *Christina Alberta's Father*, London (no date given).
[111] St. Paul, 1st Letter to the Corinthians, 12, 10.

As in the integration of the anima, there is also a *triad* when the animus is integrated. It consists of:

1. the feminine subject,
2. the masculine object (in the partner, in the real man),
3. the animus as a consciousness-transcending factor.

As the process of individuation continues, a fourth figure usually appears:

4. the archetype of the "great mother."[112]

In summary, the animus and anima are, generally speaking, the source of our empathy and antipathy. These emotional phenomena are so spontaneous that we can neither repress them nor foster them; they are beyond our conscious control and we cannot attribute them to consciously known factors. In short, they are contributions from the unconscious. From his clinical experience, Jung was able to ascertain that they are ideal images that fatally attract the sexes to each other. Ideal images have little or no connection with reality, as the victims of such projections invariably find out, to their disappointment. The projection itself usually takes place at first sight, which is why it is inexplicable. A strange feeling of "old acquaintanceship" arises: "Ah, you were in days gone by my sister or my wife" (Goethe). This romantic feeling only adds to the fascination. So we can say that almost everyone is possessed by these figures again and again, and is thus unable to see reality.

These effects of the animus and anima can be understood only if we bear in mind that our consciousness is still in the process of developing. There will always be more conscious and less conscious individuals. These differences frequently lead to misunderstandings or lack of understanding between people. Emotions come into play whenever we are unable to adapt sufficiently to the situation. The contributions from the unconscious, in this instance from the animus and the anima, can force their way through the weak spots in our persona and spoil the whole thing. We are blinded by our emotions and discussion becomes impossible. This is when our strongest prejudices thrive and flourish,

[112]Cf. E. Neumann, *The Great Mother*, Princeton, 1955.

and it can happen so quickly; one single experience is enough to trigger off the whole force of *a priori* negative judgments. Conversely, one single good experience can make us see everything through rose-tinted spectacles.

The analogy becomes clear with the effects of the complexes, as discussed in Vol. 1 of this textbook series. In the course of cultural development, however, certain collective forms of behavior have formed around the influential dominant factors of animus and anima. The collective *modus vivendi,* however, does not exactly lead to reflection on and confrontation with the unconscious, which is essential if there is to be any personal cultural development (becoming conscious). Rather it represents a prosthesis for the gaps in the persona. This keeps the background primitive and under pressure. It will then exert "grim power" in "changed form." There are still countries and continents in which, for example, the anima complex is on the first, primitive level of the mother complex, which leads to the men being totally inferior to the women.

Hence, it is not wise to wait until our relationship to the partner is distorted by our animus or anima projections. It is far less disastrous to keep these affects to oneself and to think about them in all tranquility. There will be no shortage of practice material, for night after night our dreams will keep up a steady supply. We have already listed the criteria by which a dream figure is to be taken as an animus or anima personification. In each case, the interpretation offered on the subject level (cf. Vol. 2 of this textbook series) means that we gain insight not only into our behavior in dealing with a partner of the opposite sex, but also into the constitution of our own opposite-sex subject, our own femininity (in the man) or masculinity (in the woman). Only when we know this – and it changes constantly in the process of becoming conscious – can we adjust to it properly and thus finally work out a meaningful relationship. This gives a deeper meaning to the maxim "charity begins at home"! For in psychological terms I can only really adjust and relate to the external feminine when I have really understood the internal feminine within myself.

The phenomenology of the two dominants is inexhaustible both intra- and inter-individually, so we shall stick to the common denominators (stages) given by Jung. It is on that basis that the stage of analysis attained can be judged. As the figures of anima and animus may be regarded as the actual dominant factors of the unconscious, they will always carry the hallmarks of this contamination, as defined in our typological observations in Chapter II; for example, they will bear the characteristics of the inferior attitude and functions. This means that the task is not to be underrated and is certainly not everyone's preference, for if I fail I can always ignore the psychological approach and blame the external objects; but I cannot do this when, as mentioned above, the problem lies with me and has not been solved.

We do not wish to encumber these figures of the unconscious with too much mythology. They certainly appear occasionally in every dream life. Nevertheless, we are convinced that if dreams are studied systematically, as in the analytical situation, for example, then accumulations form at certain points and these accumulations have a sort of hierarchy, one that observes the order laid down in our earlier discussion. Of course, this order is never absolute, but if the material is worked on consciously, then the whole thing becomes less diffuse. It is possible to look on this phenomenon in terms of what we referred to before as the interaction of the conscious and the unconscious. This hierarchy reminds us of the layer theory of the personality, which was discussed in Vol. 3 of this textbook series (Chapter III). As we become conscious, we participate increasingly in ever broader layers of our humanness, and this keeps us in touch with our ancestors. "What you inherit from your forefathers, *acquire* it so that you can own it." Every stage of the path, and every figure that appears enables us to communicate with the sphere of the collective unconscious, as can be seen clearly in Figure 4, p. 22, and this sheds light on the historical and mythological elements of personification listed above.

In so far as the images typified in the expressions shadow, persona, anima, animus, wise old man, and great mother come up from the unconscious, they enable us to participate in the inferior aspects of our personality. This is why these figures usually have characteristics that are relatively unfamiliar, alien, pleasant or unpleasant as the case may be, but which we have to acknowledge in ourselves and accept their existence. It is then up to our conscious to come to terms with them so that the new possibilities that are thus opened up can be meaningfully employed. These characteristics make it possible for us to cross the threshold to the previously unconscious inferior functions (and the opposite attitude). This is what we call becoming conscious. The interaction with the unconscious means that its representatives (images) or, as Jung says, its dominant factors, gradually undergo a transformation. They become less and less anthropomorphous and often emerge as more or less abstract symbols (cf. Chapter VII), which help us to integrate what had been alien before. This function of the symbols Jung called the "transcendent function."[113]

---

[113] In: C.G. Jung, *The Transcendent Function*, 1916, first published in Zürich 1957. In CW 8.

Chapter VII

Objective Witnesses

In his life, Jung, surprisingly one may say, was to come across the figure four once again. As we have seen above, this figure aided him in his functions schema, but he met it again in totally different contexts. At first it was only occasionally and somewhat tentatively, but later in the analytical process more frequent and more pronounced images appeared in the products of his patients' unconscious that reiterated the quaternity. The images were often circular in shape and divided into four quadrants. Sometimes they were four equivalent units and sometimes very complex images, which, if drawn or painted, needed to be done with great care. In such cases, with striking regularity the four components were given the four colors that we allocated to the four functions (cf. p. 57). This was the first hint as to the meaning of such constructions.

It gradually dawned on Jung that these images were a symbolic way of expressing the wholeness of the personality. It was only after years of patient observation that Jung tentatively got around to commenting on this in the publication referred to earlier (cf. footnote 42 , p. 69). This was possible because in the meantime he had come across similar representations in the so-called mandalas in India.

The noun *mandala* (Sanskrit) simply means "circle," but the images, used ritually as a *yantra,* i.e., as a basis for meditation, are almost always divided into four, like four cardinal points on a compass. As an example we can point to the chakras of Tantra Yoga, which were discussed in Vol. 3 (of this textbook series), where we also refer to the function of such systems and the aim of meditation. What we have here is a circulation or rotation of the libido with the aim of producing a sort of circle to achieve a synthetic totality. The dynamic aspect of the mandala thus hinted at is often depicted graphically as the circle revolving around its axis. The reader may recall Figure 5, p. 57 at this point.

When we observe these Indian mandalas we may be put off a little by their strangeness. But if we look around for possible parallels in the West, we soon come across structures that satisfy us both emotionally and aesthetically. We need only think of the round temples of antiquity. To surmise the psychic factor that lies behind such circular buildings as a common denominator, we must adopt as broad as possible a basis of comparison. What we then find, if we approach this openly, is that such apparently totally different objects as the lotus (chakras) and the Pyramids, from totally different ages and cultures, have had a satisfying effect on us that is almost uncanny. This is clearly the case in the prehistoric burial grounds and also later in their successors, the mausoleums. Examples would be the Taj Mahal in Agra, the so-called mausoleum of Theodoric in Ravenna or the sepulchers of the Galla Placidia, San Vitale and the renowned Byzantine churches, such as Hagia Sophia. We should also mention that the Islamic mosques also follow the principle of the same radial symmetry. Perhaps more well-known are the Pantheon of Agrippa in Rome or the later "Invalides" in Paris.

Since ancient times, the beginning and the end of human life have been depicted in buildings with the same ground plan, such as the Christian baptistries, the burial buildings we mentioned before or the circular graves from Mycenaean times. The circular pattern of birth, life and rebirth seems to find its most common expression in the symbol of the circle and the quaternity. It is no coincidence that Christian churches designed in the shape of the Greek symmetrical cross, such as St. Gereon in Cologne or St. Michaelis in Fulda, have such a satisfying effect. The popular quaternity in the crossing cupola of the domes certainly has the same significance: the pantocractor in the center, the four symbols of the evangelists in the corners (lion = Mark, eagle = John, angel (human) = Matthew, ox = Luke, i.e., three theriomorphic symbols and one anthropomorphic one) – all speak the same language. We should also bear in mind that our churches are oriented toward and related to the cardinal points of the compass. One cannot help thinking of the apparently insoluble quadrature of the circle, which the alchemists also used to illustrate the almost unattainable state of totality.[114] Birth and death comprise the totality of life and hence of the soul. It is thus no coincidence that one of its most common symbols is the *tholos*

[114]Cf. Michael Meier, Scrutinum chymicum, Emblema XXI, Francofurti 1687.

or *thymele,* the circular building.[115] This totality is identical with healing, which is why the ancient theurgic clinics (Asklepieia) all had tholoi.[116] It was not until 1966 that Boehringer found the missing tholos in the Asklepieion of Pergamon. The word *heal* is identical to the word *whole* and is also connected with the word *hale*. It can also be used with the idea of recreating wholeness, as we can read with Luther in "he (Elijah) healed the temple of the Lord, which was broken,"[117] and we have only to recall Rudolf Otto[118] to see its connection with the fascinosum.

Also of interest in this context is the ancient Roman custom of founding a city. On the chosen site a trench is ploughed in as circular a form as possible *(sulcus primigenius),* and this is where the city walls are built. In the center a quadratic hole *(mundus)* is dug out of the earth, and this is where the first offerings are placed. Then come the two main roads *(cardo* and *decumanus),* which cross at right angles in the center and lead to the four city gates. Thus the circular area is divided into four quadrants and four quarters are formed (hence the name). Once again we are reminded of Figure 5, p. 57.

As suggested earlier, there is a second part to the motif of the mandala; the transformation, the turn, the rotation, the *circumambulatio.*[119] Several of the mandalas of a ritual nature point to this, especially the Lamaistic ones. Another example is the *sulcus primigenius* of the Romans, which shows that this is the drawing of a "magic circle" serving to protect the new settlement. This rite was repeated every year in the so-called *amburbium.*[120] It should come as no surprise that similar assistance is needed if a person is to achieve wholeness. Even today we have derivatives of this custom in many places. Well-known examples in Switzerland are the exorcist rites that are still performed in Beromun-

---

[115] Cf. F. Robert, *Thymèlé*, Paris 1939.
[116] Cf. C.A. Meier, *Healing Dream and Ritual*, Daimon, Einsiedeln, 1989.
[117] I. Kings 18, 30.
[118] R. Otto, see footnote 10 , p. 29.
[119] P. Wheatley, *The Pivot of the Four Quarters: Preliminary Inquiry into the Origins and Character of the Ancient Chinese City.* London 1971.
[120] Cf. W. Pax, see earlier circumambulatio in R.A.C., Stuttgart 1957, Vol. III, p. 143 ff. Pax defines circumambulation as a "basic form of popular custom found since earliest times all over the world," l.c.
Cf. Servius, in Vergili Bucolica III, 77.

ster, Grosswangen and Sempach.[121] They closely resemble the *ambar-valia* of the Romans, except that these days Christians dispense with the *suovetaurilia* (sacrifices of pigs, sheep and oxen).

In the subjective sphere one could follow the pattern of these objective examples and say that if the personality is to achieve whole-ness it is essential to take into account all the four quarters. This occurs symbolically if the center, the objective, is illuminated from all four sides, i.e., if the full periphery of the circle is trodden. Examples of a religious and popular nature, i.e., any number of collective customs based on this schema, could be put forward from all ages and all regions, but we shall now turn to the subjective variants of the question.

---

[121] Cf. E.F. Knuchel, *Die Umwandlung in Kult, Magie und Rechtsbrauch*, Basel 1919.

Chapter VIII

Subjective Witnesses

On this subject, of course, we are obliged to become casuistic, and shall do so by producing two totally independent examples. Both cases are later phases of the analytical quest to achieve greater consciousness of the personality. Because of the striking similarity between the symbolism in both cases, we would like to compare an example given by Jung with one of our own. The first case was quoted by Jung in his Eranos lecture of 1935 and was used again in *Psychology and Religion* in 1940. The analysand was not actually being treated by Jung. The material dates back to about 1933. The patient was a very precise natural scientist, living in Switzerland and 33 years of age at the time (mid-life). The second case, one of my own, concerns a foreign professor of Experimental Psychology who had come to Zurich to train as an analyst. He was 47 years old. The two patients did not know each other. I myself saw Jung's material only after the example of my analysand was already known (March 1936).

In *Psychology and Alchemy* Jung gives the text of the vision, for a vision it is, and we should like to quote the preamble to that text here:

> All these dreams led ultimately to one image, which the patient received in the form of a sudden visual impression. He had had such fleeting images or visualizations on various occasions, but this time it was a most moving experience. As he himself said: "It was an impression of the sublimest harmony." In such a case it does not really matter what we feel or think about it. The only thing that matters is what the patient feels. It is his experience, and if it has a decisive effect on his condition then there is no point in arguing against it. All the psychologist can do is note the fact and, if he feels equal to the task, he may make an attempt to understand why this vision had precisely this effect on this person. The vision was a turning point in the patient's psychological development. Here is the text of the vision:

> There is a vertical and a horizontal circle with a common center. It is the world clock. It is carried by black birds. The vertical circle is a blue disc

with a white border, divided up into 4 x 8 = 32 parts, with a finger going round.

The horizontal circle is made up of four colors. On it are standing four little men with pendulums and round it is the ring, which was once dark and is now golden (formerly carried by the four children).

The "clock" has three rhythms or pulses:

The small pulse: the finger of the blue vertical circle jumps on 1/32 further.

The middle pulse: one complete rotation of the finger. At the same time the horizontal circle moves on 1/32 further.

The large pulse: 32 middle pulses make up one rotation of the golden ring." [122]

Now comes a second example. The text runs as follows:

One month later he can still see this image clearly, but now there is a "feminine figure behind the ball, with a veil over her face. On her right she has a staff, and with the index finger of her left hand she points to the ball with a serious expression on her face, as if to say that I should go into the ball."

In this case, too, it is easy to prove that the image is the result of a long development stretching almost over a whole year. In the material referred to earlier, Jung dealt with the idea of the quaternios, so there is no need to do so here, especially as the process is not a vital aspect of this textbook series. It is worth mentioning that the two analysands were extremely intuitive introverts. For the purpose of documenting the appearance of natural mandalas, the two images should suffice, especially as we have Jung's own commentary on the first example. However, it should be pointed out that the feminine figure appearing in the second case is a typical anima figure, pointing the way to further individuation.

A patient (whose impressive labyrinthine walk in an exceptional psychic state I described in 1939),[123] in the course of her later development constructed a three-dimensional mandala in the form of a stepped pyramid. On its four terraces were the four colors of the functions, and artistic choreographic dances were being performed there, each one

[122] C.G. Jung, Dream Symbolism of the Individuation Process, *Eranos Jahrbuch 1935*, Zürich 1936. And *Psychology and Religion*, CW 12, pp. 203f.
[123] C.A. Meier, "Spontaneous Manifestations of the Collective Unconscious," in *Experiment und Symbol*, Olten 1975.

ascending to the next step. The patient was a musician and wrote the music and choreography herself. On the top platform in the center was a golden wheel with eight spokes. Through these spokes it was possible to "look into a deep abyss." One is reminded here of Figure 4 in Vol. 3 of this textbook series (p. 35).

To conclude this brief foray into casuistry I would like to return to an objective mandala, again a three-dimensional one. It is certainly collective, but everyone has to find his way through the labyrinth of these buildings. We think of the Borobudur in Java, recalling the brilliant description given by Heinrich Zimmer.[124] It is a stepped pyramid with a side length of 120m and 40m high, making it what is probably the largest architectural mandala in existence. Technically it is the largest *stupa* (Sanskrit for "pagoda") built in Mahayana Buddhism (late Buddhism of the 8th and 9th centuries A.D. – see cover photo) and is constructed on strict geometrical lines. As a basis a round hill was marked off. On it there is a stepped pyramid with four square lower terraces and three round upper ones. On these terraces are 72 smaller stupas inside three concentric circles, surrounding the large central one. On the sides are four staircases leading off to the four points of the compass. The Buddhist pilgrim had to cope with circumambulating and climbing different parts of the pyramid, and with thousands of figurative representations (reliefs and effigies) for meditation. On the first terrace is a detailed representation of the hopeless cycle of the *samsara* (birth and death). The second terrace shows the whole developmental path of the Buddha *Shakyamuni* through the eons, until the state of Buddhahood is achieved, in other words the voluminous material of the Buddha legend and the *Jatakas* (tales of his countless incarnations). The reliefs go as far as *dharma-chakra,* i.e., to the setting in motion of the wheel of the true law (rotation). The third terrace then shows the indefatigable striving for enlightenment of the *Sudhana* (human candidate of wisdom). The model is always the *Bodhisattva,* the Buddha that is forming in its many reincarnations, and the twelve stages of the Bodhisattva path, to the *Maitreya,* the future Buddha. The fourth terrace is given to the path of Asanga, a 5th century philosopher and shows only timeless *dhyani* Buddhas *(dhyana* = inner, pure contemplation). Then come the circular terraces, with the 72 small stupas, which are open-worked and contain Buddha statues. The large bell-shaped central

---

[124] H. Zimmer, *Kunstform und Yoga im indischen Kultbild,* Berlin 1926.

stupa, however, is closed. It contains a Buddha in meditation (diamond Buddha) or *Guhyapati,* the lord of the mysteries. But the carving has been stolen. It is possible that it has been revealed or hidden by Buddha in a double aspect (Shiva-Shakti).

Thus the Buddhist pilgrim, through a series of clockwise circumambulations, moves from the lowest to the highest stage (consciousness level), always succeeding the Buddha *Shakyamuni* (Buddha on earth). At the top there occurs the resolution of the disagreeable split, caused by consciousness, into the self and the other, the world. This means that the pilgrim has arrived at the pure void in *Samadhi.* Here there is no longer any difference between the seer and the seen, etc., a state that is also attributed to the *nirvana,* which is *nir-dvandva,* that is, "without opposites." The pilgrim is assisted in this by the *Samantabhadra,* the "universal Good One," with his diamond arrowhead and the bell of mercy. Thus the pilgrim has gained access to his own, true, ineffable self. He can now say of himself: "Om, my being is a diamond, I am the very diamond of all diamond beings."

For us in the West, the idea of the objectless subject cannot be achieved (cf. Vol. 3 of this textbook series, Chapters I and IV), but for the East it is typical. We attempt to see the whole by seeing more, and we believe Schopenhauer when he says, "Always and everywhere, everything only exists by virtue of something else." But the convergence of this central symbolism over thousands of years, and in both East and West, is an undisputed fact.

Jung therefore assumes that behind all these images is an archetype, and he applies the name "self" to it. Self is a center of the personality; the radius comprises both the conscious and the unconscious systems, which is actually something of a paradox. Archetypes, by definition, transcend the conscious.

What is more they assert themselves in the course of our lives, whether we want them to or not, and they have a crucial effect on the way we live; they transcend *us.* The archetype of the self stands for wholeness, that is, the most comprehensive form of consciousness. Here in the West, however, we would not say that we had become "diamonds" if we attained this distant goal; we would tend to be more modest and simply express the hope, along with such people as Clemens Romanus, that "once we arrive there, we will be a real person."[125]

[125] Clemens Romanus, ep. in Romanos 6, 2.

Chapter IX

The Term Relationship

Oh for a glance into the earth,
to see below its dark foundations
– Faust 1.1

The most common misunderstandings concerning C.G. Jung's psychology stem from claims that it is an extremely individual, egocentric (or even egoistic) doctrine and practice. The term *individuation* may have led to this erroneous view. Criticism is rarely characterized by profound knowledge of the subject under fire. Yet we cannot think of any modern psychologist who has been as candid as Jung in offering up all his thoughts for discussion by means of his publications. In other words, it is possible to read everything and actually discover in the process that it is all data that any unbiased expert – if such there be – could easily confirm. Those who did not know Jung personally have the invaluable opportunity to have an intimate look at his personality through his memoirs[126] and letters.[127] Moreover, the reader will discover that Jung not only owed all his fundamental views to painstaking clinical observation, which may have been somewhat detached on occasion, but that he heroically worked them out and experienced them himself. He would never have recommended anything that he had not tried out himself.

We must readily confess, however, that Jung was interested only in making whole people out of himself, his students and his patients. This, of course, presupposed intensive personal work with the individual. This is where he felt his vocation lay, which is why he paid little or no attention to the current fad of sociology. What is this branch of science

---

[126] *Memories, Dreams, Reflections by C.G. Jung*, recorded and edited by A. Jaffé, Zürich 1962.
[127] C.G. Jung, *Letters*, ed. A. Jaffé and G. Adler, Olten 1972/73, 3 vols.

after all but the study of how people interrelate? The more this is done on a collective basis, however, the more the individual is ignored and violated. The smooth functioning of any community can only be achieved to the extent that every one of its members functions properly and healthily. This at any rate is how psychology views the situation and its own task. Once again we refer to the saying "charity begins at home." The man who cannot keep his stable in order will not make a good rider or riding teacher. We are not saying this is the case with sociology, but merely wish to point it out to critics who claim that Jung is not social. He is eminently social, but not on the collective level. Anyone who has not sensed his deep concern for the whole of humankind should give up searching.

Thus we feel free to declare, almost dogmatically, that the basis of all social phenomena is the individual. When two or more people form a relationship, the factors determining the outcome of this interaction are those that characterize the two (or more) people involved. Therefore it cannot be irrelevant if I am only a half person when I relate to my partner (and vice versa). Being a whole person, however, is unfortunately the most difficult, and yet also the most human of all our tasks. Seen from this point of view, group and mass psychology, and hence sociology, must be criticized for attempting to skirt the basic problem. For predominantly extroverted people this is too much trouble. But the world can no more heal itself with an attempted collective solution than it can *"am deutschen Wesen"* (with the German character) in Geibel's poem.[128] There is no alternative for us but to carry out the experiment on ourselves. And so in the remaining chapters of this book, both as a conclusion and as proof of the correctness of the Jungian approach, we shall attempt the awesome task of presenting exactly what is expected of us in a human relationship.

To examine more closely the nature of human relationships, we ought first to find out exactly what is meant by the term "relationship" or "relation." The word defines the way in which one thing is associated with another or the fact of their being so associated. In this sense, it is the basis of mathematical logic (logistics) on the lines of *Cantor* and *Frege*. With Thomas of Aquinas it is *"ordo unius creaturae ad aliam,"* which brings us somewhat closer to the psychological meaning and

---

[128] Cf. Emmanuel Geibel (1815-1884) in *Deutschlands Beruf*: "And the world may one day be healed by the German soul."

relates to our discussion of the subject/object relation in the earlier volumes of this textbook series.

Let us see what Schopenhauer has to say:

> Our knowing consciousness, which manifests itself as outer and inner Sensibility (or receptivity), and as Understanding or Reason, subdivides itself into Subject and Object and contains nothing else. To be Object for the Subject and to be our representations are the same thing. All our representations are Objects of the Subject, and all Objects of the Subject are our representations.[129]

Our perceiving subject is always the ego, and thus our ego is a conscious dimension. We can distinguish two categories of object: 1) an external object, animate or inanimate, also a thing or an idea found in the world, and 2) an internal object, for example an image, a concept or a fantasy, or even an emotional state, in so far as we perceive it.

This clarifies a little the meaning of "relation" in psychological terms, i.e., the way the subject affects the object, and vice versa. There are two basic possibilities:

a. The effect can be reciprocal or, in mathematical terms, commutative. The subject/object relation is then symmetrical.
b. The effect can be non-reciprocal, with the situation thus remaining asymmetrical.

The common examples in logic for a) and b) are:

a) Charles is the brother of Max.
b) Charles is the father of Max.

In psychological terms this means that

a) subject and object affect each other retroactively.

b) The subject only effectuates the object or the object only effectuates the subject.

---

[129] A. Schopenhauer, The Fourfold Root of the Principle of Sufficient Reason, § 16.

However, if one imagines these borderline cases in practical terms one soon realizes that there is a problem concerning the validity of case b). Is there ever really a pure case of this type, for example, when the object or subject is an inanimate (unalive) object? We assume that a psychic effectuation of dead objects is absurd, but this view is diametrically opposed to that of the world of magic; and recently there have been largely objectifiable and reproducible processes (Nina Kulagina or even Uri Geller?) that seem to be evidence of psychic interaction with dead objects. These so-called psychokinetic effects have long been largely proven in experiments (dice experiments of Louisa E. Rhine and J.B. Rhine, published in 1930 after years of verification)[130] and obviously the world of magic does not need any convincing. Hence our unavoidable "crossing of the line" has made the dead object "animate." Although we may have to dispense with incontestable physical proof of these things, we can nevertheless treat the whole subject as a worldwide view or conviction that must therefore be taken seriously as a psychological fact. This in fact recalls the situation in microphysics. It is true that when discussing "libidinous theories" earlier, we criticized the idea of borrowing from the field of physics in psychology, and for that reason we confine ourselves to analogies at this point.

In physics we speak of the distinction between the subject (observer) and the object observed. In microphysics the border between the two systems is moved more and more into the object. The result is the emergence of a reciprocal effect between subject and object that cannot be corrected (Heisenberg's principle of uncertainty). To give a clearer picture of this in human terms, one could debate the question of whether or not the air our object exhales may still actually be attributed to him. One could also say that with increasing familiarity the border between subject and object gradually blurs, so the more that we as subject want to know about the object, the more uncertain we become. Is it still the object we are observing and making statements about, or is it ourselves (the subject)? This means we are no longer dealing with a case of non-reciprocal effects, as described above. In human terms we could refer to Schopenhauer, for example, who made it clear that the criminal punishes himself through his victim. Carried to its extreme, the argument

[130] Louisa E. Rhine and J.B. Rhine, The Psychokinetic Effect, Journ. of Paraps. VII, Durham N.C. 1943, pp. 20-43.

could claim that ultimately we do not know who or what subject and object are.

Of course one is justified in asking whether we are dealing in the psychological domain with a situation comparable to that in microphysics. We have, however, seen that:

1. The uncertainty principle always applies when the distinction between subject and object is moved far enough into the object, i.e., when we enter the microstructure. An analogy is the situation in which we deal with the unconscious of our objects.

2. We have also seen that as a consequence in principle, a partial *identification* with the object inevitably emerges. What this means in psychological terms, however, is partial *unconsciousness.*

We can also see that:

3. If we pursue our examination of the object far enough, our unconscious inevitably enters. To put it more precisely: *the* unconscious comes in, for we can no longer be sure *whose* unconscious.

We should not forget that whenever we deal intensively with definite objects, projections of unconscious contents of the subject come into play as driving forces, corresponding to archetypal images. W. Pauli[131] has given convincing evidence of this in the case of Kepler. We ourselves are convinced that the attention to detail necessary in the natural sciences also, at least partially, has the psychological function of removing the myth or magic from the object. When this happens, all sorts of fascinating new facts crop up; but *instead* of the archetypal image, it is the spirit that becomes more prominent. Unfortunately this is often misunderstood today. It leads to an attitude of struggling against and controlling natural phenomena and to technicalism, i.e., to a destruction and "desouling" of nature. We are reminded here of the tragedy of Philomen and Baucis in Goethe's *Faust.*

All we are saying here is that in any situation the unconscious is contained *a priori,* for example, in the form of the fascinosum, a fact we

---

[131] Cf. W. Pauli, "The Influence of Archetypal Ideas on the Formation of Scientific Theories in Kepler," in: *The Interpretation of Nature and the Psyche,* ed. C.A. Meier, Bollingen Series 48. London: Routledge & Kegan Paul; New York: Pantheon, 1955.

referred to when discussing Jung's "subjective factor" (see Chapter I). This *a priori* containment makes it simply impossible to recognize the objective, factual situation. Those who want objective facts should either adhere to the teachings of Lao Tse, who said "those who see clearly are those who see from afar," or else simply not look so closely. Niels Bohr says the same thing when he talks about the complementarity of clarity and truth,[132] for the "objectivity" of any observation of the object – and its preciseness or intimity – are in complementary relation. We can choose one or the other, for example in the form of the experimental arrangement.

A famous example from the field of physics can easily be applied to psychology: the two theories of light as wave motion and light as particles can both be proven, the former by interference experiments and the latter by the light electric effect, for example. In the *application* of the one or the other theory, however, there can be no contradiction, for the corresponding experimental arrangements are mutually exclusive. True, one has the choice between the mutually exclusive experimental arrangements and the corresponding knowledge that has been or can be gained thereby, but this means that knowledge of the other characteristics is lost beyond recall (Bohr's complementarity). In experimental terms we have an "either/or" situation, yet in logical terms we are forced to accept that there is a "not only/but also" situation.

Let us take note of the fact that no description of phenomena is independent of the nature of the observation. Of course this has long been known in psychology, but we feel that not enough account has been taken of the uncertainty principle. This is understandable when we bear in mind the awkward paradox this leads to: the more intensively we deal with an object, especially a human being, the more inevitably we will partially identify with him. The inevitable outcome of becoming as conscious as possible and of making factual situations conscious is thus the impossibility of distinguishing clearly between subject and object. Yet *discrimination* is the classic criterion for consciousness and *identification* for unconsciousness. (We are reminded at this point of Empedocles in the 5th century B.C., and his two powers of *neikos* [contention] and *philotes* [amiability] – the separative principle in the cosmos and its opposite.) Only where there is consciousness can there

---

[132] Bohr here deliberately refers to Schiller's poem 183, Spruch des Confucius (1799).

be awareness of differences in characteristics, and only then are opposites felt as such.

The famous example of this is the dream, in which the most inconsistent and contradictory factual situations are possible without this bothering us during the dream. The so-called dream ego lacks discrimination, the classic characteristic of the ego. It is only when the dream is recalled, i.e., when the waking ego makes the dream a content of the conscious, that we are struck by these inconsistencies – in other words, only when the "perceiving subject" (Schopenhauer) discriminates between subject and object. Only from the point of view of the conscious is the dream a product of the unconscious! We refer here to the Samkhya teaching that the contamination of soma and psyche is responsible for all the suffering in this world and all illness.[133] The paradox we refer to is that any further growth in consciousness inevitably entails a partial increase in unconsciousness. Through Jung, we now have in psychology the further step of "interpretation on the subject level" (cf. Vol. 3 of this textbook), for this necessarily unconscious aspect of the situation will consequently and necessarily be reflected in dreams.

It seems to us, however, that what is much more important about these observations, on a practical level, is the fact that they force us to admit that whenever we interact with another person, we can never be really sure of *what* we are doing to him. The fatal connection between subject and object naturally starts with a simple *conversation*. This fact is so obvious it hardly seems worth mentioning, and yet we are unlikely to be fully aware of its fundamental significance. It does, however, remind us of the *responsibility* we are shouldering, whether we want it or not, and this amounts to a demand for the highest possible degree of consciousness. At the same time we accept that at most all we can do is to prevent the most obvious projections from coming into being. For other reasons as well, absolute consciousness is not possible, and moreover would not help us to avoid the problem of the indeterminacy principle.

While conversation can be dismissed as a banal situation, the consequences are much more serious when things *happen* without conscious intention or action, i.e., in cases of pure projection. The expressions *coup de foudre* or "falling in love" speak for themselves in this respect.

---

[133] Cf. C.A. Meier, *Healing Dream and Ritual.* Daimon Verlag, Einsiedeln, 1989.

In such cases, when one does not recognize the projection, the effect is automatically exteriorized. The effect can be seen, but the cause, because it is unconscious, seems to be missing. This is why the cause is posited in concrete form, for example, Eros and his arrow.

There seems to be something helpful about illustrating what intrinsically cannot be illustrated. We are then the "innocent" victim of a deity or daimon greater than we are. In Plato's *Symposium,* Eros is a "mighty daimon." His arrows *(tela passionis)* are the equivalent of the projectiles we project. With this notion we shift the responsibility for our projection onto an impersonal power. This attempt at exoneration may well be healthy from a psycho-hygienic point of view, but unfortunately it becomes invalid once we have uncovered this process in light of the above knowledge. True, it is not our conscious that has given rise to the projection, but it is certainly our unconscious, and we can no longer fully disclaim responsibility for this. We shall return later to the rather delicate question of ascribing responsibility.

It is safe to assume that so-called telepathic effects are regarded these days as absolutely real effects, even though they do not meet the conditions of time and space and even though we have no field theory to explain the *actio in distans.*

Clinical observations of active projections of all kinds led Freud to speak in certain cases of *transference.* Let us take a closer look at this term. One can distinguish among various categories of transference phenomena:

1. *Transference of affects:* when we get worked up and shout at someone, he will get worked up, too. The same thing applies to a friendly encounter, of course. It is true that what we have here is an automatism, but the process is a causal one, for the angry words are the cause and the affect is the effect. This well-known contagious effect of emotions can be observed in other gregarious animals (e.g., hair standing on end among hyenas as a danger signal).
2. *Participation mystique:* we have greater difficulty in understanding what lies behind primitive ceremonies. Let us take as an example the Atninga ritual with the natives of Central Australia (Arunta), as observed by Spencer and Gillen.[134] When a punitive expedition is

[134] B. Spencer and F.J. Gillen, *The Native Tribes of Central Australia*, London 1899, p. 461 ff.

organized, all the participants must drink blood, and their bodies are sprinkled with blood so that they become supple and active *(utchuil-ima)*. We would say they do this to achieve the necessary affective mood. The older men decide whose blood shall be taken and nobody dares to refuse, even though considerable amounts of blood are often involved. The drinking of blood is a way of preventing any form of betrayal. If any member refuses to drink blood, it is forced down his throat, with apparently the same effect as if he had drunk of his own free will. We would say that the Arunta posited the blood as causa, but in our eyes it is not, and so we unthinkingly speak of superstition or resort to references to suggestion or autosuggestion. We overlook the fact that the participants have shared in a blood communion, produced causally by the ritual, a ritual that as such has a very clear effect.

We can join Lévy-Bruhl[135] here when he talks of "participation," a phenomenon he claims is inseparably linked with every mystical practice. With Jung we find the expression "participation mystique." It is based on the presence of what Lévy-Bruhl called *"représenta-tions collectives,"* which in themselves have a mystical character. This is the same phenomenon that the German ethnologist A. Bastian[136] called *"Völkergedanken"*– folk thoughts – and they are closely related to what Jung called archetypal images. These notions create a rapport between myself and my objects, and thus with others too, and this rapport has a definitely mystical character. With the native Australian there is, thanks to this rapport, a *communio* in that each individual is, for example, a reincarnation of an *ancestor* from the Alcheringa period. By belonging to a specific dead person he "participates" with all the other dead men or the dead animal. Should he unwittingly eat the flesh of this dead animal, he himself will die if he finds out the truth; thus everything is mystically interrelated. Better known is the relationship of the black man with his bush soul, or the Bororo Indian in the state of Mato Grosso in Brazil, who is utterly convinced he is an Arara (red parrot).[137] Of

[135] L. Lévy-Bruhl, *Les fonctions mentales dans les sociétés inférieures*, Paris 1910.
[136] A. Bastian, *Der Völkergedanke im Aufbau einer Wissenschaft vom Men-schen*, Berlin 1881.
[137] Cf. Karl von den Steinen, *Unter den Naturvölkern Zentralbrasiliens*, pp. 305-306, Berlin 1894.

course, we do not need to go into the bush to find such mystical-magical relatedness. We need only recall the total relatedness between portrait and model, as in Oscar Wilde's *The Picture of Dorian Gray* (1891), or G.B. Shaw's *Pygmalion* (1912) and H. de Balzac's *La Peau de Chagrin* (1831).

The "causality" at play here is *post aut iuxta hoc, ergo propter hoc.* Time as simultaneity is thus given a mystical significance, as is space. The cardinal points play an important role, and spatial distance can be disregarded. In all these cases we can help ourselves by believing we perceive a purely "psychic causality." But the question is whether we give these things greater justice by taking up the "extraordinary force" of a Melanesian or a Manitu.[138]

The problem becomes even more blurred with a third category of transference phenomena, which follow similar lines.

3. *Totemism:* Let us take the example of the Intichiuma rituals among the natives of Central Australia.[139] These are extremely complicated procedures that must be carried out to the letter if the totem animal or plant is to flourish, i.e., if the native is to be given life. The concept of "psychological causality" does not seem to have much meaning here, for how can the animals or plants in question respond to the positive attitude of totem members by becoming more fertile? We must confess that even assistance from the unconscious is not much help here, although there is no denying that as a result of the ritual, the libido of the Arunta is channeled into the totem – in other words, is "transferred" there.
4. *Projection:* Freud's term "transference" is basically intended to convey a special form of the projection of unconscious contents, as observed in the course of analytical treatment. The patient "sees" his father in the analyst, for example. Freud proved this is the projection of an inner father image. The expression "transference" is a literal translation of the term projection and is intended here to indicate an unconscious displacement of the subjective contents onto the object. But one must always be able to prove that these are one's own

[138] Cf. Arthur O. Lovejoy, The Fundamental Concept of the Primitive Philosophy, in: *The Monist*, La Salle, 1906, pp. 357-382, esp. 381.
[139] Spencer and Gillen, l.c. cf. fn. 134, p. 134.

contents, and this is where the analytical method is useful. The great difficulty, however, is in trying to understand that such projections can really affect the object. We could mention, for example, the popular German word for lumbago, which is "witch's shot."

There are interesting ethnological examples: the medicine man of the North Californian Indians has at his disposal so-called icicles, which he carries in a leather bag. By rubbing them, he can "charge" them and then shoot them so they hit a man he has been commissioned to maim, make ill or even kill (magic). Once it has done its job, the icicle is shot back to the medicine man and is still dangerous. Thus the medicine man has to protect himself, which he does by standing in front of a tree when he sees the icicle returning. At the last moment he jumps behind the tree, and the icicle penetrates the bark of the tree, where it can be easily collected. It must now be calmed down and rendered harmless, which happens once again by rubbing, and then it is returned to the leather bag.

The psychological interpretation of this impressive spell thus works on the assumption that active projections can have an objective effect. We also learn that projections have a boomerang effect; in other words, they recoil back on us. On this point Jung is reminded of chemical reactions, which result in the alteration of both bodies. At any rate, here, we see the principle of *actio = reactio,* but it is as puzzling to us as the case of the *cloth trees.* This is a healing practice still popular in the Balkans, especially in Yugoslavia, and probably influenced Freud in his choice of the term "transference." A sick part of the body, a wound or a sore, has a cloth wrapped round it. After the cloth has soaked up the "illness," it is hung in a tree. Thanks to its boundless vitality, the tree easily copes with the illness and the patient is healed.[140] In other words, the illness is transferred to the "cloth tree" – a classical example of folk etiology. What is exciting about these archaic cases is that they have been rediscovered in modern psychology in connection with "transference" in the analytical sense. It is by no means rare for a patient to suddenly lose a troublesome symptom while at the same time the therapist notices abortive signs of this symptom in himself. However, thanks to the fact that he is better equipped, i.e., has a stronger consciousness (having acquired it in coping with similar problems

[140] Cf. P. Kemp, *Healing Ritual*, London 1935.

during his own analysis), the therapist soon deals with the situation. To help understand such odd effects, it is advisable to think of Jung's principle of synchronicity, for we view these effects as "acausal coincidences."[141]

A particularly impressive example of this sort of transference is presented thoroughly in the casuistry of Robert M. Lindner (†1956) under the name of Kirk Allen.[142] The patient was an atomic physicist, and in carrying out his work he fell into the "hole" of the unconscious and developed a complicated fantasy system with which he identified (hallucination). Dr. Lindner was infected by this, whereupon the patient gave up his hallucinations and had to "dig out" his own doctor from the same "hole."

To return to an everyday level, it should be pointed out, for example, that our reaction correspondingly alters when someone has certain expectations of us or has prejudices about us, be they positive or negative. This effect occurs even if we are completely unaware of these factors, even if (or because) our partner also knows nothing of his projections. The fact remains that our reaction changes and only then, only afterwards, do we become aware of the strange situation.

The situation reminds us that our attitude toward a certain object can change without our actually doing anything about it ourselves – for example, after we have dreamed about it; this is true even if we cannot remember the dream. Of course, such a situation remains fully within the subject, which is why it appears comprehensible. It is a phenomenon we feel we understand on the basis of the principle of causality, assuming we acknowledge the reality of the unconscious.

An element remains that refuses to be resolved so easily. Let us take an example from Francis G. Wickes.[143] The only son of an overprotective mother had run off. The mother went into analysis, and one day she suddenly had the illuminating idea that she had to live her own life, instead of living for her "lost son." At that very moment the clock in the consulting room struck 12. Three days later she received the first and

[141] Cf. C.G. Jung, Synchronicity: an Acausal Connecting Principle, CW 8. German original, 1952.

[142] Robert Lindner, *The Fifty-Minute Hour*, New York 1955. *The Jet-Propelled Couch*, pp. 221-293.

[143] Francis G. Wickes, Three Illustrations of the Power of the projected Image, in: *Studien zur analytischen Psychologie C.G. Jungs*, Zürich 1955, pp. 247-263.

only news from her son. "I am sitting on a hill 3000 miles away from you. I have just heard the clock strike 9, and suddenly all my fear has gone. I'm coming home." The time difference between 12 o'clock and 9 o'clock local time actually meant that the two events happened simultaneously. This raises the far-reaching question of the range of the unconscious, reminding us of the unlimitedness in space and time of telepathic phenomena – something totally beyond our comprehension.

Let us mention one further peculiarity of the effects of the unconscious, this time something related to death rather than to life. The following observation was made by Wolfgang Kohler:[144] A man is asleep in his hut and dreams he is in the next village, where he commits a crime that incurs the death penalty. Next morning he talks about the dream. It turns out that such a crime had actually been committed in the next village at roughly the same time. The man is accused and confesses. He is executed. What is going on here is described in our terminology as total identification with the projections of the group.

At this point it is worth thinking about the various forms of the *a priori* category of causality, as distinguished in the Scholastic philosophy of the Middle Ages, which owed much to Aristotle. Thierry of Chartres (approx. 1140 in Paris) and much later Thomas Aquinas (1225-1274) distinguish the following four categories of cause:

1. *Causa efficiens,* which is said to be the externally operating cause. Unless there is *causa efficiens* there can be no effect. It stands in a hierarchical effect relationship with the *primum movens,* or the *causa ultima* = God.
2. *Causa finalis* – the final cause – explains the purpose of a change.
3. *Causa formalis* – the formal cause – is the architectural plan, shaping the matter.
4. *Causa materialis* – manifesting cause in the area of substance.

To our modern scientific way of thinking, only the first of these four – *causa efficiens* – is valid today, so we can no longer actually accept a type of thinking operating on the principle of *causa equat effectum* (like begets like). For us the formal element no longer has any connection with causality.

[144]W. Köhler, in Amer. Journ. Psychol. 50, Worcester USA 1939, p. 271 ff., esp. p. 273.

We are now entering the sphere of the sympathy doctrine, which Theophrastus, for example, saw as the cosmic interrelatedness of all things, the *sympatheia ton holon* (the sympathy of all), which was also the basic concept of the Stoics (Marcus Aurelius and Poseidonius). I have been informed by H.R. Schwyzer that the term *sympatheia* is itself Platonic, as can be seen in Tim. 30 b, d and 32 b. The *sympatheia rerum,* as well as the related doctrine of signatures,[145] assume a sort of causal relationship, based on the similarity of the two positions. *Causa formalis* and *causa efficiens* are equal here or interchangeable; in fact the causal principle in the strict sense of the term is abandoned in favor of the formal principle. One can also say that a simple, formal coincidence stands for causality. This view is at the root of many popular ideas and concepts, especially in the field of folk medicine. Eduard Renner, a medical doctor, tells us that in the Canton of Uri, for example, the water left over after a sort of turnip has been boiled is used to cure illnesses of the respiratory tract. As they are being boiled the turnips make a sort of rattling sound, just like the person suffering from respiratory troubles, and the reason it is regarded as a cure is precisely because of this similarity *(similia similibus curantur).*

The same formal principle of similarity is behind many forms of what is known as "magic by analogy." For example, in times of great drought the Indians send a mother into the cornfield with her infant baby so that the rain will come. Their reasoning is that a baby is a never-ending source of wetness and therefore that meteorological wetness (rain) is bound to follow soon.

These applications of the *causa formalis* raise the idea of the contagiousness of the shapes of objects. Bearing in mind the observations made earlier about effects on "dead" objects and the distinction between subject and object, one could say that such practices "animate" the "dead" object, so that it begins to behave like the subject (magic by analogy). We are also reminded here of the well-known phenomenon of the "pitfalls of the object" described to us so vividly by Fr. Th. Vischer.

As all our examples show, what is happening or is reputed to be happening, goes beyond what we, acting on conscious conviction, usually understand by causality. Nevertheless, there is no denying the presence of these convictions and their effects. If we wish to understand them as such, then we are forced to conclude that apparently there is an

[145] Cf. Scott Buchanan, *The Doctrine of Signatures*, London 1938.

unconscious that is everywhere identical, i.e., betrays the same characteristics at all times and in all cultures – characteristics that have almost
completely disappeared for Westerners. If we do come across such
phenomena, we immediately dismiss them as superstition, which re-
lieves us of the worry of having to think about them seriously. We have
created innocent branches of science for them, such as ethnology, and
we have lexicons, such as the invaluable *Handwörterbuch des deutschen Aberglaubens* [Handbook of German Superstition].[146]

But the psychologist is very interested in the existence of a sphere of
the soul that is spaceless and timeless. He recalls, for example, the
Platonic world soul.[147] It is the first creation of the demiurge and
contains the world inside itself as a body. Through its power of self-
activation it is also the *moving force* of the world. But the world soul is
also the source of *apprehending,* for it is a link between idea and
manifestation, consists of both, and thus can apprehend both. It is the
most perfect and most judicious soul of world totality, as a living being.
These Platonic conditions relate to the concepts of the Vedas (Upanishads), where the Brahma assumes the same position as Plato's world
soul. It is the divine all-one, the eternal, unchangeable being that is the
basis of all things, and with which the Atman as metaphysical self is
ultimately identical.[148]

In the Stoa, the all-animating *pneuma* takes this position, and according to the evidence of St. Augustine,[149] the Manichaeans also had a
world soul.

In Neo-Platonism the idea of the world soul once again played a
significant role. A good example would be Plotinus (207-270 A.D.) in
The Enneads IV. 3, 8,[150] who holds that individual souls are born of one
soul and are interrelated through sympathy or antipathy. Although later
the notion of the world soul gradually loses significance, its traces can
be detected to varying degrees in such authors as Marsilio Ficino (1433-
1499), who produced the first translation of *The Enneads,* Agrippa von

---

[146] H. Bächtold-Stäubli / E. Hoffmann-Krayer, *Handwörterbuch des deutschen
Aberglaubens*, 10 vols., Berlin 1927-1942.

[147] Cf. Plato, *Timaios*, 34 sq.

[148] Cf. R. Reitzenstein and H.H. Schaeder, *Studien zum antiken Synkretismus.
Aus Iran und Griechenland*. Leipzig/Berlin 1926.

[149] Augustinus, de vera religione IX.16.

[150] Plotinus, The Enneads, IV., 3, 8. There is a critical edition in Plotini opera,
ed. Paul Henry and Hans-Rudolf Schwyzer, 3 vols., Bruges 1951-1973.

Nettesheim (1436-1535), Pico della Mirandola (1463-1494), Paracelsus (1493-1541), Cardano (1501-1576), Patrizzi (1529-1597), Campanella (1568-1639), for whom the world soul is still regarded as God's instrument, and Robert Fludd (1574-1637). For Giordano Bruno (1548-1600), world soul and sympathy still hold a central role. For J.B. van Helmont (1577-1644) it has magnetic effects, which are very similar to sympathy. Even with Bacon (1561-1626) the notions of sympathy are still important, as is the case with Shaftesbury (1671-1713) and Berkeley (1684-1753). The idea also preoccupied Goethe and Novalis, as well as Schelling, Hegel and Friedrich Creuzer (1771-1858), who was responsible for a first edition of Plotinus (Oxford 1835). Leibniz's "pre-established harmony" is also to be seen from this perspective. Swedenborg had visions about this, as did many romantic philosophers.

Generally speaking, however, it must be stated that by the 17th century the idea of the world soul and sympathy had completely disappeared, to be replaced by "ether" and the growing importance of measurements, quantity and proportions. At the same time, in the light of the natural sciences, the psyche became increasingly more subjective and developed into a consciousness psychology. This was still the case in the 19th century. Only recently have we come back, through Jung, to the rediscovery of an *objective psyche,* namely the *collective unconscious,* which can be viewed as a sort of return to the *anima mundi* and all its long-lost qualities.

Returning to the subject of incomprehensible effects, we can point out that since 1952,[151] with his working hypothesis of *synchronicity,* Jung has offered us a third possibility for fully realizing that this is a reality to be taken seriously. In cases where the classical-causal approach breaks down, in that the space-time parameters break down, we can assume that what now operates is a generic "similarity of pattern" between subject and object (cf. magic by analogy, countertransference). This is a somewhat vague, abstract concept, defined in intellectual terms, which posits an arranging or constellating factor.

This "similarity of pattern" has the same quality as "archetypal images," whereas the arranging factor (A) corresponds to the archetype itself. Through the "similarity of pattern," for example, between subject and object (a and b), images have a parallelity that we see as a connection through similarity of meaning, although these terms are

[151] C.G. Jung cf. fn 141, p. 138.

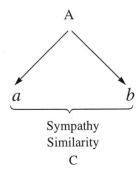

based on a formal principle. We recall at this point the cases of Lindner and Wickes referred to earlier. If we speak of projection or transference in such cases, then this is a special way of observing the similarity of pattern from a point outside it (C). We do this on the assumption that in a magical procedure, for example, *a* is the active partner and has illusions about *b* (e.g., in the transference). This would mean that *a* and *b* are partly identical or unconsciously identical, i.e., undifferentiated or indistinguishable. In this, *b* can be both active and inactive. We have already stated that when we fall in love, for example, we automatically produce an image, such as Eros with his arrows, which serves as a quasi-causal representation of the non-representational constellating factor, A. This description seems to us more satisfactory than the pure projection theory, which works asymmetrically on the assumption that the unconscious psyche of *a* has projected something onto *b*. But this assumption does not cover the whole of the phenomenon, as can be seen clearly when 1) the illusions of *a* have no correspondence in the subject (when there is no hook for the image to hang on), or 2) when there is no definable object corresponding to these illusions, so that it must still be created, i.e., is summoned (Eros).

The clearest examples of this are the well-known countertransferences. While theoretically simple, in practice they are incredibly complicated, as we know from the common occurrence of two people being in love with each other. We can see that even antiquity satisfied this need for symmetry by placing *Anteros* alongside Eros. An altar was dedicated to him, together with Eros, in the old gymnasium at Elis.[152] The corresponding legend is found in Themistios.[153] Anteros avenges unre-

---

[152] Pausanias VI, 23, 3.

quited love as Alastor (the spirit of revenge), in whose name there is an altar in Athens[154] and who is the son of Mars and Venus.[155]

Relief representations of the struggle of Eros and Anteros from Nitrodi (Ischia) can be seen in Lidia Furti, "Rilievi dedicati alla Ninfa," in *Rendiconti Acc di Arti, Lett. Belle Arti,* Vol. XXVI, Napoli, 1951. The subject is also relevant from the point of view of transference and countertransference. Dante has Francesca say, *"Amor ch'a nullo amato amar perdona"* (D.C. Inferno V, 103).

The lack of differentiation between subject and object is, of course, the result of mixing unconscious elements. This recalls the paradoxical conclusion that any new consciousness initially involves partial unconsciousness. This blending of conscious and unconscious elements is known in psychological terms as *contamination* (Lat. *contamino* = pollute), and any new consciousness contents are always contaminated. This is why the most difficult and most important task of consciousness is *discrimination,* although by definition this is never fully achieved.

In this connection, reference should also be made to another common expression in psychological terminology: *constellation.* What we usually understand by this are all those latent, unconscious elements of our psyche which, because of a given situation, are placed in an "activated state" and thus, to a certain extent, tend to cross the consciousness threshold, i.e., are "prepared for action." Let us return to the previous example; when a young man gets to know a young woman, then the possibility of falling in love is "constellated;" it is "in the air." Actually it is in both people or also "in the stars." *Stella* is Latin for "star." Constellation is an expression for our star *images,* which are simply specific *arrangements,* and one can wonder who did the arranging. They are actually purely statistical groups, which we alone can arrange into specific images and can see; and there are probably gestalt psychological reasons for this. But what emerges is that we have always traditionally seen them as divine images or, as Jung would say, archetypal images. This obviously brings up the question of projection. Projection can only come from us as people and is thus asymmetrical. However, as we saw earlier, the action of projection always leads to reaction. We also see projection in the form of belief in the stars, where

[153] Themistios, Or. XXIV, 304 ff.
[154] Pausanias I, 30, I.
[155] Cicero, de nat. deor. III, 23.

the projection has an effect on the projector (horoscopes). This process can be seen clearly, for example, in the *Metamorphoses* of Ovid, where the hero is placed in the firmament (apotheosis), thus satisfying the need for symmetry (see diagram above).

Here, too, an *objective entity* is required that *transcends* the subject. Belief in the stars makes clear our "illusions" about an object in the absence of anything objective corresponding to these illusions. What does exist is a totally neutral vehicle the stars as projection carriers. The fact that the stars seem so far away has a calming effect, for this makes us feel unthreatened by overpowering, divine forces. In this respect Plato put forward an even better radical psychological theory. He asserted that these images – we could call them archetypal images projected by us – are not even in the stars but are much farther away – even more abstract – and are actually pure ideas that exist far beyond the visible firmament, beyond the heavens.[156] (Paradoxically, psychoanalysts might see in this an early form of resistance to the (collective!) unconscious.)

Let us return to the more down-to-earth case of two people in love; here the situation is obviously a symmetrical one with acknowledgment of Eros and Anteros. The partners are connected by sympathy, which literally means similar suffering, although the similarity is often merely assumed to exist. From a theoretical point of view, they would go back to a common constellating factor. If Eros is one-sided, however, then we have a case of asymmetry, and the substratum of the projection does not fit into the equation. As it is not present, i.e., nothing corresponds to it in the object, we are all the more inclined to *place* it there. As a consequence we are the helpless victim of a supernatural power, wounded by the *telum passionis* of Eros, suffering but without the compassion, the sympathy, of the partner. Eros then remains relatively impersonal and conceptual, which has been more and more the case in recent times, with the result that the dimension of Eros these days is little more than that of sexual hormones. It is now regarded as outdated to think in such poetic images as Eros with his arrows, and in fact it would no longer be appropriate if the "mighty daimon" is viewed only in terms of hormones. We seem to have forgotten all too quickly the cosmogonic significance attached to Eros in the Orphic religion. There he is the offspring of the union of Nyx and Chaos (darkness and void),

---

[156] Plato, Phaidros 227 C.

out of which comes the shining silver world egg, which again in turn produces Eros as a creating, shaping force and a great god. The whole body of theological and philosophical poetry of those times revolves around him. In Pherekydes, Zeus changes to appear as a demiurge (world creator) in Eros.[157] We are reminded of the role of the *philotes* (love) in Empedocles, where the *sphairos* (sphere) recalls the Orphic world egg. Even with Sophocles neither the great gods nor mere mortals escape Eros, and when Antigone says, "I am not here to hate you but to love with you,"[158] we should take this to heart, today more than ever before. But with Plato, Eros is still the mighty daimon[159] even though he is the king of the gods,[160] and Plato devotes a whole main dialogue to him. In this dialogue we find the words, "God lives in him who loves,"[161] pointing unmistakably to the transcendental dimension. By the time we get to the Romans, however, Eros is no longer autochthonic, existing simply as *Eros funéraire* on sarcophagi.

In this respect, we living in modern times are even worse off. Anything erotic is taken personally, and we say, "*I* have fallen in love," on the assumption that it is a personal decision, and yet the verb *fall* does in fact suggest that it is an accident. This secularized approach is undoubtedly an unhealthy metamorphosis of the original concept. It is probably by way of compensation that we have exalted Eros and sex on films and television. When Christianity altered the equation love = God into God = love, it preserved the transcendental aspect but deprived it of much of its original force and immediacy.

So far we have distinguished between two types of projection:

1. Projections that are reducible to unconscious qualities belonging to the subject. Causality is more or less satisfied. Such projections are symmetrical.
2. Projections where reduction (1) is not possible, so that the projection process is not reducible either, which means that causality is not satisfied. Thus an asymmetrical situation.

---

[157] Pherekydes, Procl. in Plat. Tim. 368.
[158] Sophocles, Antigone 523.
[159] Plato, Sympos. 203 A 3.
[160] Plato, ibid. 195 B 6.
[161] Plato, Sympos. 180 B.

In the second case it is inadvisable to attribute the contents to the subject, for this would give rise to the risk of *inflation.* The powerful contents of the unconscious image could overwhelm the ego. A splendid example of this is the bourgeois Mr. Primby, who imagines himself the Assyrian King Sargon II, King of Kings in H.G. Wells' *Christina Alberta's Father.* [162] The difference between the two types of projection is that, unlike the second, the first type is actually necessary and is in fact healing, in the sense of making *whole.*

In the case of pure projection (2), a *genuine symbol formation* occurs. According to Jung, a symbol is the best way to describe a relatively unknown quantity, whereas Freud claimed it produces lack of clarity in something that is well-known. On the matter of "unknown," we would say the situation described in the symbol does not belong to the subject either, an important fact from a psychohygienic point of view (cf. Mr. Primby, above). This makes the genuine symbol extremely useful as regards personality development. We only rarely, and never fully, accept that we are often the objects or victims of forces that transcend the subject. This is a purely psychological observation that we make without having to believe in stars or demons.

Initially it is difficult to understand the idea of being affected by forces that are not contents of the subject, either conscious or unconscious. We can only guess at their existence and imagine that we feel them, but we do not understand them. From a cultural and historical point of view, however, they are very familiar. Plato himself gives serious thought to the religion of the stars, but he also rejects hypostases in favor of pure images.[163] In our approach, the star religions from Babylon and Egypt personify specific forces that are superhuman in dimension. They become relatively human only in our *internal* planet system, in the planet gods and especially in the planet children. In this way a psychology *sub specie aeternitatis,* i.e., without consideration of local or temporal conditions, was built up in later antiquity. This is worth comparing with Macrobius' *Somnium Scipionis,* which was discussed in Vol. 2 of this textbook series. With the passage of time, this psychology of the firmament becomes more and more detailed, and the decanate star images are brought in to help in this, as are the fixed stars that lie above and below the zodiac *(paranatellonta).* As seen in the

[162] H.G. Wells, *Christina Alberta's Father*, London, no date.
[163] Plato, Phaidros 247 C.

frescos in the Palazzo Schifanoia in Ferrara or the "Salone" in Padua
(Palazzo della Ragione), this late antiquity-Hellenistic-Roman tradition
was revived during the Renaissance. This interest, and the extensive
ancient cult, in turn naturally gave rise to repercussions in the form of
compulsion by the stars, Heimarmene or *Ananke* (necessity), in other
words, fate. It is seen in more abstract, genuinely ancient, terms in the
Moiras or Fates. These powers must be seen in connection with the
concept of freedom, for they form its compensation, i.e., its limitations.
Compulsion by the stars, fatalism, means that falling in love is something we suffer and that the phrase "making love" is an inaccurate one.
Virgil has an apt comment to make on this *(quisque suos patimur manis
exinde per amplum mittimur in Elysium).*[164] When Schiller has General
Illo say to Wallenstein, "In your bosom are the stars of your fate,"[165]
this sounds somewhat euhemeristic compared to the pious acceptance
of fate in antiquity, even though there is some truth in it in modern
psychological terms. Wallenstein has to be torn free from his inhibiting
belief in the stars and from his astrologer Seni.

It is acknowledged that these forces shape the myth, in special cases
the astral myth, or, more exactly, that they present themselves in the
myth. The myth, if one understands it properly, then shows how one can
best deal with these forces, and is therefore therapeutic, especially in
avoiding inflation. And as Jung has shown, it also provides us with a
further opportunity to develop our personality, which is a way of
shedding light on the real meaning of our individual lives. Here we shall
let Jung speak for himself:

> Hardly had I finished the manuscript when it struck me what it means to
> live with a myth, and what it means to live without one. Myth, says a Church
> Father, is 'what is believed always, everywhere, by everybody'; hence the
> man who thinks he can live without myth, or outside it, is an exception. He
> is like one uprooted, having no true link either with the past, or with the
> ancestral life which continues within him, or yet with contemporary human
> society. He does not live in a house like other men, does not eat and drink
> like other men, but lives a life of his own, sunk in a subjective mania of his
> own devising, which he believes to be the newly discovered truth. This
> plaything of his reason never grips his vitals. It may occasionally lie heavy
> on his stomach, for that organ is apt to reject the products of reason as

[164] Virgil, Aen. VI. 743 f. We all suffer from our own demon, / Only then can
we pass into Elysium.
[165] Schiller, Die Piccolomini 2069.

indigestible. The psyche is not of today; its ancestry goes back many millions of years. Individual consciousness is only the flower and the fruit of a season, sprung from the perennial rhizome beneath the earth; and it would find itself in better accord with the truth if it took the existence of the rhizome into its calculations. For the root matter is the mother of all things.

So I suspected that myth had a meaning which I was sure to miss if I lived outside it in the haze of my own speculations. I was driven to ask myself in all seriousness: 'What is the myth you are living?' I found no answer to this question, and had to admit that I was not living with a myth, or even in a myth, but rather in an uncertain cloud of theoretical possibilities which I was beginning to regard with increasing distrust. I did not know that I was living a myth, and even if I had known it, I would not have known what Sort of myth was ordering my life without my knowledge. So, in the most natural way, I took it upon myself to get to know 'my' myth, and I regarded this as the task of tasks, for – so I told myself – how could I, when treating my patients, make due allowance for the personal factor, for my personal equation, which is yet so necessary for a knowledge of the other person, if I was unconscious of it? I simply had to know what unconscious or preconscious myth was forming me, from what rhizome I sprang.

Jung wrote these words in 1950 in the foreword to a new edition of his early work "Transformations and Symbols of the Libido" (1911).[166]

From this we can clearly see just how important is the "constellating factor" to the growing consciousness of the subject, i.e., of its object; for there is a meaning relationship between the two. This is why a large part of Jung's later work is devoted to investigating this significance of myths. We emphasize at this point, however, that here once again what is important is the symmetrical relationship between our consciousness (and these apparently spontaneous images) and the process system of the unconscious. Our conscious participation is bound to have an effect on the way these myths work. Any further development of personality is thus dependent on whether or not we are capable of establishing a conscious relationship to the contents of the unconscious that appear in this way.

We therefore postulate the thesis that any *genuine relationship* is ultimately dependent on consciousness. In psychological terms, the value of a relationship is dependent on the degree of mutual consciousness. In fact one can speak only in terms of a relationship when it is not

---

[166] Jung, Symbols of Transformation, CW 5, originally published in German as *Symbole der Wandlung*, Zürich 1952.

based on total or partial identification, projection or transference, for these phenomena are founded on the admixture of unconscious material. In short, we can also say that it fundamentally depends on *who* is related to *what*.

This finally brings us to the end of the unfortunately somewhat complicated theoretical prerequisites for our subject of human relationships. We shall now go on to deal with examples demonstrating the thesis that relationship is dependent on consciousness. This thesis excludes all those "relationships" that do not fit, that is, unconscious relationships based on partial consciousness in relation to the object. But as this is by far the commonest type of relationship, we cannot exclude them from the discussion, but must treat them as if they were the natural preliminary stages of conscious relationships in our sense of the term.

So-called "primitive" societies provide typical examples of "unconscious relationships," for here the relations between members of the tribe, even marriages, are still quite conventional. They are based on total identification. For example, we know of cases where the medicine prescribed for the husband is also taken by the wife and children, and where a urine sample requested by the doctor is given by the whole family. R. Moffat has many similar examples of family identity.[167] A bushman, whose son refuses to obey him, complains, "The fellow is going around with my body and blood and won't obey me!" A very widespread custom, one that used to be found in ancient Judaism, is that the soul of the dying father is transferred to the son with a kiss. Any cult of ancestry is an indication of this identification with the forefathers, and of course it is to a certain extent justified genetically as well.

Along the same lines there is the common custom of teknonymy, the naming of the parent from the child. E. Crawley[168] offers the following examples from Central Australia: "After the birth of the first child, father and mother take on the child's name. If the child is called Kadli, then the father is now called Kadlispinna *(spinna* = suffix for father) and the mother is called Kadlingangki *(ngangki* = suffix for mother)." D. Livingstone tells the same about the Batswana in Africa. After the birth of her son Robert, Mrs. Livingstone was called "Ma Robert,"

[167] R. Moffat, *Missionary Labors and Scenes in South Africa*, London 1842.
[168] E. Crawley, *The Mystic Rose*, 2nd edn., London 1927, Vol. II, p. 190.

instead of Mary as before.[169] For obvious reasons the identification is particularly strong with relatives, and it is interesting to note that in English the synonym for *relatives* is "relations." There are even some very odd effects stemming from the fact that every member of the family, including the cat and dog, is caught up in the same unconscious milieu. This means there can be no consciousness either of one's own or of others' motives, so that these motives are then projected. The best examples are the notorious marital quarrels due to unconscious identification. The Babylonian confusion of tongues as an etiological myth is not always adequate as an explanation here. The classical example of a relationship is that between man and woman, especially in marriage (cf. Chapter X).

The above observations have been made on the assumption that the syzygy underlies marriage as the archetypal arranging factor. Bearing in mind the myth of Aristophanes in the Symposium, the objective of marriage would be to create, or rather to restore, a mystic unity between the somehow related opposites of man and woman. If we take a look at the institutions that have been set up to achieve this objective, we can soon see that they cannot have been worked out rationally, but are rather "arranged" according to an archetypal background and, in a sense, preexist. In our opinion this can be seen clearly in the primitive marriage-class systems. English authors in particular have investigated these incredibly multifaceted and complicated social orders; for example Sir James George Frazer[170] has written four volumes, Ernest Crawley[171] has produced two, and John Layard[172] has written about the nearly indescribably complex situation in Malekula (New Hebrides), where he spent many years.

The simplest schema is the well-known Sister-Exchange Marriage, traces of which still linger on even in our day: a man marries the daughter of the brother of his mother, i.e., the female cousin on his mother's side. His sister then marries the brother of his wife (that is, the male cousin on the mother's side) (cf. the diagram in Figure 6). A remnant of this type of marriage was preserved in Ireland at the beginning of this century: when a girl loved a young man, they managed

[169] D. Livingstone, *Missionary Travels and Researches in South Africa*, London 1837, p. 126.
[170] J.G. Frazer, *Totemism and Exogamy*, 4 vols., London 1910.
[171] E. Crawley, *The Mystic Rose*, 2 vols., London 1927.
[172] J. Layard, *Stone Men of Malekula: Vao*. London 1942.

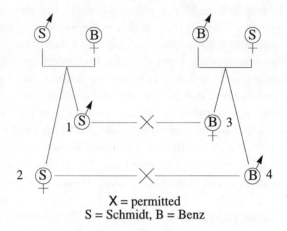

Figure 6. Sister-Exchange Marriage

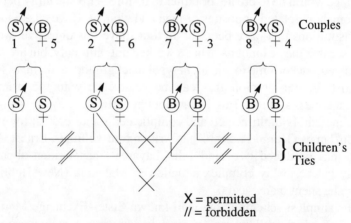

Figure 7. Cross-Cousin-Marriage

to pluck up enough courage to say to each other, "I wish you were my cousin." Cross-Cousin Marriage (cf. the diagram in Figure 7) is much more complicated. The union of the children of two brothers or two sisters is forbidden; what is permissible is the marriage of the children of a brother with the children of a sister.

These rules and regulations are made even more complicated in that further dichotomies are introduced and the individual groups are divided into "moitiés" (halves). Of course, all these systems are a great hindrance to the contracting of marriage. The idea behind all this must obviously be to prevent incest. But at the same time it forms a compromise with the endogamous libido, the kinship libido, by setting up the legitimate relations of the marriage classes. Whereas the kinship libido would make us want to unite with our "relations," this is prevented by these marriage classes, which amounts to a check on incest on the physical level. This is essential for culture to develop and continue, for incest – that is, the union of like with like – can never produce anything new, except children. This prevention of incest on the physical level forces us to realize it on the spiritual level, which is probably one reason why incest is performed by gods and kings *(hieros gamos).*

Again we recall the *Symposium,* where Plato has the woman Diotima, the priestess-anima, say:

> Now those who are teeming in body betake them rather to women, and are amorous on this wise: by getting children they acquire an immortality, a memorial, and a state of bliss, which in their imagining they 'for all succeeding time procure.' But pregnancy of soul – for there are persons who in their souls still more than in their bodies conceive those things which are proper for the soul to conceive and bring forth; and what are those things? Prudence, and virtue in general; and of these the begetters are all the poets and those craftsmen who are styled inventors."[173]

However, if we think about the motivation for the marriage classes of the "primitives," it seems from our perspective that these people already had a consciousness of cultural requirements. But this cannot be the case. We must rather assume that they have a sort of "pre-consciousness" that "knows" all these connections and acts in accordance with them by setting up these systems. The systems themselves, however, represent a powerful compulsion, which gives these relationships a highly impersonal stamp, with the result that such marriages exist on a conventional level, apparently to serve biological purposes.

We somehow sense that very *personal* relationships can be *dangerous,* and this is certainly one of the reasons for the ups and downs that are so common before and after people get married. A person is on the point of becoming involved in the closest possible relationship, and lo and behold, the *discrimination* thereby entailed is already making its presence felt. For if our assumption is correct, that a genuine relationship depends on consciousness, then this consciousness calls for differ-

---

[173] Plato, Sympos. 208 E – 209 A.

entiation (discrimination). In other words, there must also be a *negative relationship*. Once again, the so-called primitives had a way of dealing with this, as we can see in an example from South Australia. When a child is born in the Narrinyeri tribe, the father gives the remains of the umbilical cord *(Kalduke)* to a man from a neighboring tribe. As a result of this "transference," the children of the two men become *ngiangiampe,* i.e., they must not have physical contact with one another, or even converse. Thus the identification or communion involved in ownership of the Kalduke is a negative relationship. This relationship is simply established by the institution and performs the dual function of separating and uniting, for oddly enough, these same children must organize the trade and communication between the two tribes.[174] This is an undertaking that is not without danger and is best conducted on an impersonal level.[175]

Ethnologists are agreed that primitive married couples did not have a personal relationship. In fact a personal relationship is just not possible where everything is so strictly laid down. What is interesting from a psychological point of view is that this same conventionality as regards marriage is also found on a higher level. In royal families, at least until fairly recently, the question of personal likes and dislikes was simply not a factor in the question of marriage. The decisive factor as to whether or not a union was suitable was purely and simply the higher interests of the collective.

[174] E. Crawley, *The Mystic Rose*, II, p. 143 ff.
[175] Ibid. I p. 287 f.

Chapter X

Marriage as the Paradigm for Relationships

We should like to begin by giving our reasons for having chosen marriage as the classical example of human relationship. The initial premise is that the feminine for man and the masculine for woman embodies that which is both the most intimate (the human) as well as the most unknown (opposite of consciousness). These two facts lead to maximum attraction (fascination) and rejection (discrimination). When these opposites reach a high potential, which is bound to happen in the close togetherness of married life, they present an excellent opportunity for growth in consciousness, for both partners are inevitably in a situation where they have to come to terms with each other. This is a very demanding procedure, one that can be borne only if the moral responsibility thereby involved is taken seriously. Growth in consciousness stands or falls with this. Without this there cannot be a genuine relationship, in the above sense of the term, nor can there be a parallel process of individuation. Thus marriage is the perfect institution in this respect, providing that it is not abandoned at some point as "broken down." From this point of view, the indissolubility of marriage, which is advocated by the Church for religious reasons, also has a psychological function, assuming, that is, that both partners are serious about the idea of personality development. If we accept this thesis, then the institution of marriage is the only corner into which we are pushed, in the interests of becoming ourselves, without being able to retreat to or to escape from the situation. This gives it its unique value for the individuation process and hence for the ability to form genuine relationships.

We shall now attempt to discuss the marital relationship in these terms by looking at some fundamental principles.

1st basic rule

Our consciousness is always only partial. Its main contents are affect-toned to varying degrees, depending on our age.

It is in the nature of things that with young people there are large areas that are still unconscious. (There are still many experiences to be had.) But according to the above observations, as long as we are unconscious, we cannot form relationships. Thus the relationship between young partners can be only a partial one. What is striking here is that the stronger the feeling of being in love, the greater the degree of unconsciousness. That is why the relationship is all the more felt as fatal compulsion, for obviously there cannot be an element of *free* choice, since that would presuppose lucid consciousness. Yet we must exclude the idea of a compulsive *"relationship,"* which can continue in the complete absence of the feeling of being in love, as is the case with dependence or subjection, which is a much more difficult situation. Thus, according to these observations, a total relationship is something we can expect to find only in older people.

2nd basic rule

By way of contrast, falling in love is still a common occurrence with young people and thus must be regarded as normal. Since higher consciousness is as yet only a long-term objective, the question arises as to what replaces it in the case of young people. It is reasonable to assume that the immediate objective or preliminary stage is the biological one. Fortunately we can still hope that the choice of partner at this stage takes place purely instinctively and unconsciously, for the unconscious seems to operate with a natural accuracy. On the whole, Nature seems to ensure the most favorable combination of qualities when it comes to the preservation of the species.

But what unconsciousness means in every relationship is non-differentiation, i.e., at least partial identity. A consequence of this is the well-known fact that one partner presupposes in the other the same psychological structure, the same interests, the same sexual functioning and feeling. In other words, there is an illusion of unity which seems to create "one heart and one soul," harmony and happiness. But this unity is anticipatory and taken for granted, which is why such "happiness" is very fragile. This risk is usually compensated for by the fact that the unconsciousness is perpetuated as long as possible. This is not difficult, for it is a *return* to original unconsciousness, which, far from being a struggle, is actually pleasant. This is why one often sees childish gestures in young lovers. Psychoanalysis has coined the term "thalassal regression" to express this. It can be understood as the incestuous wish to return to the mother's womb, into what Jung describes as "the teeming depths of an as yet unconscious creativity?"[176] The last-mentioned fact explains why people become very poetic at this stage. It is a stage which performs a given function at a given time, which is why Jung says the following:

> It is, in truth, a genuine and incontestable experience of the Divine, whose transcendent force obliterates and consumes everything individual; a real communion with life and the impersonal power of fate. The individual will for self-possession is broken: the woman becomes the mother, the man the father, and thus both are robbed of their freedom and made instruments of the life urge.[177]

In this phase we are still within the bounds of the instinctive goal, and thus collective, so that we cannot yet speak in terms of a personal conscious relationship.

It is possible to examine the conditions that modify the way such "relationships" come about in accordance with a series of different factors:

A) Parental influence

First and foremost *parental influence* affects the choice of partner. We said earlier that the choice of a husband or wife is influenced by instinctive, unconscious motives. The young man's relationship with his mother and the girl's with her father is a crucial factor in the way they create a *type* of partner. The Greek word *typos* means "coinage," or rather the process of coining, as is the case with coins themselves. The coining is the consequence of what Konrad Lorenz calls "innate release mechanisms," which only operate in the formative years, i.e., in youth, and their effects can never be eradicated. J. Lhotsky goes so far as to equate the "innate release mechanisms" with Jungian archetypes.[178]

---

[176] C.G. Jung, Marriage as a Psychological Relationship, CW 17, p. 193.
[177] Ibid. p. 192.
[178] J. Lhotsky, Der Begriff "Prägung" in der vergleichend-analytischen Psychologie. Beiträge zur Sexualforschung, 6. Heft, Stuttgart 1955, pp. 57-67.

In terms of Complex Psychology we would say that the choice of spouse is determined mainly by the *imago* of the parent of the opposite sex, i.e., through the image of the subjective relationship to the object – the son to the mother, the daughter to the father. If this image has a positive emotional tone, it will influence the choice in an encouraging way, but if it has a negative tone, then it will impede the choice. For example, when a daughter consciously has a positive attitude toward the father, then she will automatically, quite unconsciously, look for a man like her father. If the tone of the father imago is negative, then it can make the choice difficult, for it easily leads to hostility toward men in general. A simpler consequence, however, is where the partner must embody the opposite of the father. The situation is much more complicated when the negative father attitude leads the daughter to feel hostile toward men in general. As the negative father imago is unconscious (negative father complex), it has the famous characteristic of all complexes, that is, it assimilates *further* contents (cf. Vol. 1 of this textbook series, p. 180 ff.). The result is then resentment of authority, dogmatism, rebellion, so that the woman herself acquires a certain masculinity. By way of contrast, if the daughter hero-worships her father, she may find it impossible to find a man who would be a marriage candidate. The father has been placed on a pedestal and nobody can hold a candle to him. It should be borne in mind, however, that behind such a positive father complex there lurks the *unconscious of the father himself* who, for his own purposes, cultivates and abuses the daughter's love. He needs to become more clearly aware of his own anima problem! The parallels for the son with a positive or negative attitude toward the mother (positive or negative mother complex) can easily be derived from the above remarks; what is more, they have been brilliantly described by Jung in his Eranos Lecture of 1938.[179]

What we are dealing with is how the relationship problems of the parents can affect those of the children. It is very common for parents to be unconscious of their own problems, with the result that they are simply passed on to the next generation. This can develop into a real family tradition; the most impressive examples are found in the tragedies of antiquity, such as Tantalides and the curse of Atreus. This means that the parents actually shape the *fatum* and thus incite their offspring

---

[179] C.G. Jung, Psychological Aspects of the Mother Archetype. *Eranos-Jahrbuch, 1938.* CW 9, Part 1, 1959, Archetypes and the Collective Unconscious.

to commit matricide or patricide. Such a situation is due directly to the fact that a person unconsciously behaves in an artificial way in relationship with the partner. For example, when a mother does not work through her problems with her husband, i.e. represses them, with the "noble" motive of wishing to maintain appearances and not upset the child, she ties her son even more firmly to her apron strings as a substitute for her husband. In doing so, her unconscious pseudo motive is that she wants to bring up her son to be a better husband. If such a son does not become homosexual or a Don Juan, then the only sort of woman he will dare approach will be one who is far beneath the mother, so that she cannot be a "threat" to his mother image. The alternative is a woman who completely tyrannizes him so as to tear him away from his mother. Francis G. Wickes' *The Inner World of Childhood*[180] gives impressive examples of this unconscious influence of the parents. The vicious circle is broken only when *one* link in the chain musters up the courage to look matters in the face.

From this we can derive a third basic principle: What the parents do not live out, but leave unconscious or repress, has to be lived by the children as compulsion, that is in a negative form. The impression one has is that they have to compensate for all that has remained unfulfilled in the lives of their parents. Common examples are the good-for-nothing children of excessively moral-minded parents, or the ambitious sons of idle fathers.

B) Typological determinants in the choice of partner

The powers of attraction or repulsion between two people know no bounds (positive or negative fascination). From a psychological point of view, love and hate are simply reciprocal. Typologically there are two possibilities for the attraction:

a) Either one looks for the same things in one's partner, on the principle that "birds of a feather flock together," or
b) one seeks and loves what one does not have oneself, for only that has value.

The first option (a) probably comes about because one cannot understand anything that is different. In the second option (b) we are

---

[180] Francis G. Wickes, *The Inner World of Childhood*, New York, 1927.

reminded of the discussion between Socrates and Diotima in the *Symposium:*[181] Eros, as the son of Poros (Resource) and Penia (Poverty)[182] seeks the good and the beautiful (Kalokagathia), for he does not possess either[183] and is filled with longing for both.

The "same plus same" formula (a) would seem initially to have a better chance of materializing, because the "totally different" formula (b) is disliked. But the latter can actually exert its own fascination as the mysterious and the incomprehensible. Moreover, a) has the disadvantage of offering nothing new, except in the biological sphere. Thus the choice between a) and b) is geared to the question of whether one is looking for something new or merely the confirmation of oneself. The motives for the decision remain unconscious, manifesting themselves only in irrational sympathy or antipathy.

The *introverted person* will seek to create a relationship to the outside world through his partner and so his choice will fall on someone who is extroverted. This can in fact be very beneficial, for example in terms of his reputation in the world, but initially it will not be a relationship in the psychological sense. The extroverted man, for example, will by way of contrast, seek a relationship with his background in a woman who puzzles him, and the extroverted woman will seek it in a "spiritual" man.

So far we have looked at the situation in terms of its significance on the external level. Yet what does it mean in terms of the development of the personality, which amounts to differentiation of all four functions? So long as the inferior opposite function and the opposite attitude are experienced externally through projection, i.e. in the partner, they cannot be differentiated. Now if someone has an opposite type as a husband or wife, then the question arises as to what significance this situation has on the inner level.

We know that with the introverted type the "subjective factor" plays the most important role. Thus with him the partner becomes a foil against which the "subjective factor" is experienced. Initially the partner is not even perceived as an opposite, for he is unreflectively presupposed to have an identical experience. This projection fits in with the well-known tendency of women to indulge in acting or mimicry.

---

[181] Plato, Sympos. 200 D.
[182] Ibid. 203 C.
[183] Ibid. 201 D.

With the extroverted type a similar adaptation is going on by means of *introjection* of the image of the partner, and this can even go so far as identification. What is meant by the term introjection is the adaptation of the object to the subject by means of empathy. It acts here as an adaptation process. In both cases the projection (introverted) or the introjection (extroverted) of the opposite leads to an "imagined" adaptation of the partner, which gives rise to a "possessive attitude," resulting in a pseudo wholeness.

Now according to our 7th fundamental principle (cf. Vol. 3 of this textbook series), there comes a point in life when the attitude changes. This means a crisis in that the previously existing modes of adaptation to the partner (identification, introjection, projection) become impossible. These crises should be viewed as life's claim to consciousness, which would then remove some of the sting. Initially the result of the crisis is 1) boredom with the extrovert and 2) incomprehension with the introvert.

As a result of this 1) the extrovert seeks his opposite elsewhere, usually outside, for he wants a *change*. Being simple himself, he now begins to seek complicatedness; and 2) the introvert seeks *understanding*, again usually outside.

Simplicity is what he is after, being himself complicated. It goes without saying that in both cases this seeking for something different is bound to lead initially to a rejection and alienation of the partner, which amounts to a negative realization of difference and variety.

C) The scope of the personality as a determinant in the relationship

Jung felt he was able to observe that in most marriages both partners also take opposite positions in another connection.[184] He advocates that we distinguish between 1) the container and 2) the contained partner in a marriage.

Jung describes the "container" as being the more complicated, many-sided, contradictory, problematical, often divided personality, with many facets, inhabiting many rooms. By way of contrast, the "contained" is simpler, like a straightforward six-sided cube; he inhabits, as it were, just one room, and that is where he is "at home."

---

[184]C.G. Jung, cf. fn 176, p. 157.

We are reminded of a very apt and amusing example from the field of zoology. It was long thought that a certain type of sea worm, *Bonellia viridis,* only existed as a female. The animal is about 1m long and has at the back a small sack a few centimeters long. It was not until 1912 that the zoologist F. Baltzer (Bern) discovered that that was where the male of the species was to be found. He is just 1mm long and spends his whole life in the Fallopian tube of the rather large female.

Returning to the human sphere, we can say that the "contained" is completely surrounded by the "container," and in this way a great deal of experience is available to him. A contained woman, for example, is wholly contained spiritually in her husband, and a contained man *(Bonellia* type) is wholly contained emotionally in his wife. Both live entirely *within* the marriage, which may look ideal in its undividedness, but of course this situation has the disadvantage of total mutual dependence.

The container, on the other hand, is bound to continually disturb the other's simplicity for the very reason that he himself is not contained; in other words, he is permanently "outside" the marriage and feels himself to be complicatedly problematical. The more the contained clings to the status quo, the more the container feels excluded.

From this perspective, too, we are presented with a natural possibility for the development of the personality during the mid-life change. The one who was previously the container now begins to seek his counterweight in the form of undividedness, of being contained. The one who was previously contained now has occasion to take a look at the other rooms, i.e., to see and understand himself in his complicatedness (inferior function and opposite attitude). The security that he used to seek in the container he must now seek in himself. In doing so, he will discover within himself the complications which the container had sought in him in vain. With this change of perspective, the container develops a greater yearning for simplicity and has to accept it as genuine. He must accept his complicatedness as self-division. Only then can his nature fight against it and make possible the integration of an undivided self which he had previously vainly sought outside himself. Jung has the following remarks to make about these transformations:

> This is what happens very frequently about the midday of life, and in this
> wise our miraculous human nature enforces the transition that leads from
> the first half of life to the second. It is a metamorphosis from a state in which

man is only a tool of instinctive nature, to another in which he is no longer a tool, but himself: a transformation of nature into culture, of instinct into spirit.

One should take great care not to interrupt this necessary development by acts of moral violence, for any attempt to create a spiritual attitude by splitting off and suppressing the instincts is falsification. Nothing is more repulsive than a furtively prurient spirituality; it is just as unsavory as gross sensuality. But the transition takes a long time, and the great majority of people get stuck in the first stages. If only we could, like the primitives, leave the unconscious to look after this whole psychological development which marriage entails, these transformations could be worked out more completely and without too much friction. So often among so-called "primitives" one comes across spiritual personalities who immediately inspire respect, as though they were the fully matured products of an undisturbed fate. I speak here from personal experience. But where among present-day Europeans can one find people not deformed by acts of moral violence? We are still barbarous enough to believe both in asceticism and its opposite. But the wheel of history cannot be put back; we can only strive towards an attitude that will allow us to live out our fate as undisturbedly as the primitive pagan in us really wants. Only on this condition can we be sure of not perverting spirituality into sensuality, and vice versa; for both must live, each drawing life from the other.[185]

D) Archetypal images as determinants in the relationship

This subject takes us to the most complicated sphere of the relationship problem. The archetypal images of the opposite sex that lurk behind the choice of a partner are necessarily unconscious, which is why they are automatically projected onto the partner. They are anima or animus images. Before embarking on a discussion of these determinants, let us recapitulate what we said at the beginning about marriage being the prototype of a relationship. We stated that the archetype of the syzygy is responsible for this, that is, the divine couple as one.

We shall therefore proceed to the 4th basic rule, which states that every man carries within him the eternal image of woman, and that every woman has her inborn image (or images) of man.

We recall here the Platonic myth referred to in footnote 80, p. 99, or the prince and princess in fairy stories. And let us not forget that the opposite sex is initially the unknown, but for this very reason becomes the exponent of the unconscious opposite. Because images of the anima

[185] C.G. Jung, ibid. p. 197.

or animus are usually human figures, they embody contents that can be assimilated in the psychological sense, and are thus capable of forming relationships.

To sum up some of the characteristics of the *anima:*

> sphinx-like character, ambiguity or equivocation; an indefiniteness that seems full of promises, the inscrutable smile of the Mona Lisa, both old and young, mother and daughter; dubious chastity; childlike helplessness combined with apparent knowledge.

The animus has the following characteristics:

> ambiguous hero role; his words should not be too clear so that a lot can be read into them. He himself is misunderstood, so that one can be understanding and self-sacrificing about him. One thinks here of *Gösta Berling* (1891) by Selma Lagerlöf (1858-1940), where the Cavaliers, a group of men, are a fitting reminder of the multiplicity of the animus (cf. p. 165 in the German text).

As stated earlier, projection of these images onto real people usually leads to passionate attraction. Initially it is the contained one who projects onto the container. The reverse is somewhat different, in that the container initially projects "into the air." Understandably this makes the contained rather uncomfortable, for sooner or later the "right" sort of woman is going to pass by or a man is going to shoot past in a sports car. Such a woman can easily become a *femme fatale.* And yet it can happen that because of the projection, *something* in her carrier that was shadowy before acquires firmer outlines, so that the one casting the projection brings about in the object something that would otherwise not have had much chance to develop (*femme inspiratrice*). Many a man has achieved his true potential in this way. This, however, is rather the exception. The thing about such projections is that sooner or later they end up with mutual disappointment. This is because ultimately the problem of the animus or anima is a *drame intérieur* which should not be acted out outside. Its real *aim* is rather to provide a link with this other side of ourselves, for anima and animus are the key figures in our real unconscious; they are its actual exponents, their personifications. At the fourth and fifth stages of the anima development (see above), these figures thus often have something angelic about them. This link to the unconscious is by no means easy to produce, however, because the unconscious is very different from anything that our conscious knows (inferior function and attitude). As we are firmly convinced that this link to our own unconscious, to our inner self, is a vital prerequisite for any real relationship in the psychological sense, both with the partner and the environment, we would like to attempt to make more of it.

Following Jung, we have attempted by means of a diagram to acquire a certain overview of the extremely complicated relationship between man and woman.[186] We shall present it here, albeit in a simplified form (Figure 8).

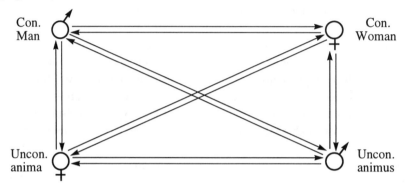

Figure 8

All the arrows represent possible relationships between the two partners, partly on the conscious, and partly on the unconscious level. They are to be regarded as reciprocal, in accordance with our assumption of action and reaction of the two systems. This means that in fact we are dealing with four systems. If there is to be a total psychological relationship, they are all indispensable and inescapable. They produce a quaternio, something we discussed previously in another context. In other words, a man can have a total relationship with a woman in the external world only if and because he is related to his own inner world. This relationship includes the whole environment, of which the real woman is a part. The diagram can be extended upwards into "the big, wide world," where the relationship function (anima, Eros) will have tangible effects for the man.

[186] C.A. Meier, "Individuation und psychologische Typen" in: *Experiment und Symbol*, Olten 1975, p. 193 ff.

This brings us to a fifth basic rule: as regards the ability to form relationships, only someone who has a good relationship with himself can relate properly to an object.

Self-knowledge is clearly not only a formidable challenge but also the basis of genuine religion and philosophy, a fact that has been known since Thales and which could be read in the Apollo temple in Delphi. What it means today, more specifically, is that in addition to the conscious one should also get to know and accept the unconscious. Only then do we understand the true meaning of the words in Leviticus 19:18,[187] "Thou shalt love thy neighbor *as thyself*" (as also in Luke 10:25-37).[188] The question of how to go about loving oneself is not an easy one. St. Augustine was preoccupied with this problem in CDI, 20. And we all have problems with such contents as the shadow. But if we do not manage to live in peace with ourselves then this can easily lead to our loving others just because we cannot love ourselves. But this sort of love never brings happiness. The only legitimate way to love oneself in the right sense is rarely practiced because there are pleasant and tried and tested methods of avoiding the issue: "loving" others is regarded as highly commendable, and these days it seems sufficient to love one's work. It is possible to delude oneself, when it comes to self-awareness, through daydreams and pleasant fantasies. Another popular conceit is a spurious interest in "higher things," which are thus given erotic overtones. People who do this are particularly repulsive to those not involved, for in fact their behavior only conceals "self-love" in the worst sense of the term. One of my medical chiefs used to call such ladies "charity hyenas."

By way of contrast, the real Eros as a relationship function par excellence comes into effect only when one knows *what* one loves and *with what* one loves – in other words when one is aware of *who loves whom.* We are fully aware of the extent of this challenge, but in the light of the above remarks there is no getting out of it, even if it makes real love a rather uncomfortable challenge. Even Ovid shared this view, as can be seen from the following verses from the "ars amatoria":

> Qui sibi notus erit, solus sapienter amabit

> (Only he who knows himself will love with wisdom – a.a. II, 501), and:

---

[187] Lev., 19, 18.
[188] Luke, 10, 25-37.

Quod latet, ignotum est: ignoti nulla cupido (What remains hidden is not known: what one does not know cannot entice one – a.a.III, 397).[189]

A remark of Leonardo da Vinci's (1452-1519) seems to confirm what we have said: *"nessuna cosa si puó amare ne odiare, se prima non ha cognition di quella"* (Nothing can be loved or hated unless it is known). Freud seems to reject this and comments:

> That is to say: One has no right to love or hate anything if one has not acquired a thorough knowledge of its nature. And the same is repeated by Leonardo in a passage in the treatise on painting where he seems to be defending himself against the charge of irreligion: 'But such carping critics would do better to keep silent. For that [line of conduct] is the way to become acquainted with the Creator of so many wonderful things, and this is the way to love so great an Inventor. For in truth, great love springs from great knowledge of the beloved object, and if you know it but little, you will be able to love it only a little or not at all....'
>
> The value of these remarks of Leonardo's is not to be looked for in their conveying an important psychological fact; for what they assert is obviously false, and Leonardo must have known this as well as we do. It is not true that human beings delay loving or hating until they have studied and become familiar with the nature of the object to which these affects apply. On the contrary, they love impulsively, from emotional motives which have nothing to do with knowledge, and whose operation is at most weakened by reflection and consideration. Leonardo, then, could only have meant that the love practiced by human beings was not of the proper and unobjectionable kind: one *should* love in such a way as to hold back the affect, subject it to the process of reflection and only let it take its course when it has stood up to the test of thought. And at the same time we understand that he wishes to tell us that it happens so in his case and that it would be worthwhile for everyone else to treat love and hatred as he does.[190]

We can recognize in these words of Freud the theory of sublimation, from which the genius Leonardo was "excused." The Renaissance Platonists, however, had a more unadulterated understanding of Leonardo's words because he was open to the appearance of a transcendental factor, a divine element in Eros. It is certainly more beneficial for us to consider what lies behind love apart from the biological aspect. We have already seen that the syzygy as archetype refers to *divine*

[189] trans. D.R.
[190] S. Freud, Leonardo da Vinci and a Memory of his Childhood, CW 11, p. 81.

figures, and the *Gnosis Theou* (awareness of God) has always been regarded as the aim of human awareness, with love playing a crucial role here. Seneca wrote: *"deum colit qui novit,"* God is worshipped by those who know him."[191] Cicero is also of the same opinion;[192] both of them probably base their views on Poseidonius. We should also recall here St. Paul's diatribe against the "unknown God" on the Areopagus hill at Athens.[193] Our views on Eros are largely supported by Marsilio Ficino (1433-1499) in his *Commentary on the Symposium* and in the *Theologica Platonica,* and by Pico della Mirandola (1463-1494) in the "Heptaplus." At this point we would like to take a closer look at a particularly interesting discussion on the subject, which we owe to the Sephardic Jew Leone Ebreo (Jehuda Abrabanel or Abarbanel, (1460-1530). It is to be found in his book *Dialoghi d'Amore.*[194] Let us begin with a passage where he echoes Leonardo without actually mentioning him:

> Love must be preceded by knowledge; for we could not love anything we had not first known as good. And we cannot have knowledge of anything before it is actually in being. As our mind is a mirror and model, or more exactly, an image of real things, so there is nothing we can love until it exists in reality. We desire only such things as we have known as good. (I, pp. 6-7)
>
> Increase of love comes with increase of knowledge. And love of God is ever united with ardent desire: namely, to gain whatever we lack in knowledge of God; so that the increase of our love keeps pace with that of our knowledge. For as the nature of God infinitely exceeds human knowledge, and as His goodness no less exceeds the love man can bear Him, so they nourish ever a happy desire, as ardent as limitless, to increase evermore their knowledge and love of God. For such increase is always possible in respect of the Object of such knowledge and love. (I, p. 35)

[191] Seneca, Ep. 95, 477.

[192] Cicero, de nat. deor. II, 153.

[193] Apg 17. Cf. also Ed. Norden, *Agnostos Theos*, Leipzig 1912/ Darmstadt 1956. A more recent discussion of this question is to be found with Elisabeth Michel, Nullus potest amare aliquid incognitum. Ein Beitrag zur Frage des Intellektualismus bei Thomas von Aquin. (Studia Friburgensia, Neue Folge 57) 1979.

[194] Leone Ebreo, *Dialoghi d'Amore*, Roma 1535. Modern ed. Carl Gebhardt (Bibliotheca Spinoziana, tome III), Heidelberg/London/Paris/Amsterdam 1929. Translated into English by F. Friedeberg-Seeley and Jean H. Barnes, Soncino Press, London, 1937. The page numbers are from the English edition.

And as wisdom is far broader and deeper than the human intellect, he who strikes out the farthest into its divine ocean has a greater knowledge of its width and depth and a greater desire to arrive at those shores of perfection which are within his reach. Its waters are like salt water, for the more a man drinks, the thirstier he becomes. (III, p. 312)

In other words, love grows as knowledge grows.

Again it is undeniable that love presupposes knowledge; yet it does not follow from this that love is the ultimate activity of the soul. (I, p. 48)

In this way the perceiving soul is raised above itself and united with the deity. This development becomes apparent as Sophia gains more and more significance in the course of the Dialoghi. In our terminology she represents a later form of the anima (5th level). She is placed above physical love, without this physical love being excluded or depreciated.

And as Plato shows, love is a desire of that which is made pregnant of beauty to give birth to it in the likeness of the father; and such is the love not only of the mind but of the body. (III, p. 373)

Thus with Ebreo we get an interesting cycle, a *circolo amoroso,* whose ultimate objective is a sort of coniunctio of body and soul (anima).

The Arabs make the universe to be a circle, the beginning of which is God; and from Him a continuous chain of being descends to first matter, which is the most removed from the Divinity, and there the circle turns and ascends through the various degrees of being until it reaches the point of origin, to wit, divine beauty, with which the human intellect is finally united. The Arabs teach that love descends from the summit of the angelic world to the nethermost point of the lower world, and thence ascends to its first origin, passing successively from one degree of being to another, with wondrous order and in the form of a circle with a point of origin marked on its circumference. (III, p. 335)

The first half circle of being is born and created out of the highest being, and descends from the greater to the less, down to the nethermost degree of chaos or first matter, and in the other half circle returns from the lesser to the greater, to the source whence it first issued. (III, p. 450)

We feel that there is an analogy here to our demand that the shadow should be attended to first. This motif is dealt with at great length in alchemy, under the heading of chaos, *prima materia,* etc.

It can be clearly observed here that the anthropological notion of the principle of love is replaced by a cosmological one. The world becomes an organism, a macranthropos, whose unity is created and guaranteed mythically and mystically by love, which makes the world go round. Love is ultimately identified with God and at the same time represents the highest form of relationship with God or the *Gnosis Theou.* Thus what this makes possible is nothing less than the *deificatio in statu amoris.* Plotinus would speak here of the soul becoming one with the One. Once again it is easy to recognize behind this cosmogony or rather anthropogony the syzygy motif (father = first intellect; mother = chaos).

> The two first begotten of God in the creation of the world, viz., the first intellect which is resplendent with all the Ideas of the supreme Creator, and this is the father, the former and generator of the world; and Chaos, dark with the shades of all the Ideas, and containing all their essences, and she is the mother of the world. (III, p. 305)

What is more the whole thing is reminiscent of the *Empedocles* fragments quoted earlier. The condition of the cosmos, the all-round being, when it is united in Eros, tends to separate into several parts in hatred, and comes together in One through love. The only thing is that with our Jewish-Platonic author, the *primo e unico motore* has been reduced to this love, which, in the ensuing cyclical process (Figure 9, below), operates as cosmogonic, i.e., anthropogonic Eros. It is not easy to see just how far Ebreo is following Proclus with this image. At any rate, there is a very similar concept in Proclus' *Commentaries on Plato's Timaeus*[195] and in his *Elements of Theology,*[196] where reality descends hierarchically from and imitates a single highest principle, the One.

The whole is a "stream of love," *circolo amoroso,* in which those who truly love each other join in.

With this Neo-Platonic image we have suddenly moved deep into the cosmic sphere, but actually we are no longer talking about a simple projection but about a genuine symbol formation. Ebreo's experiment fits in beautifully with our thesis that a genuine relationship in the best psychological sense is based on the principle of wholeness and all-inclusiveness, which unites all opposites through a creative achieve-

[195] Proclus, in Tim. I. 210, IIff.
[196] Proclus, Stoicheiosis Theologike, 206-209, cf. E.R. Dodds, *Proclus, The Elements of Theology*, Oxford 1933, pp. 180-183.

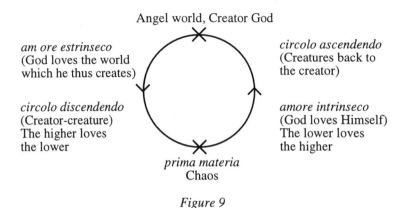

Angel world, Creator God

am ore estrinseco
(God loves the world
which he thus creates)

circolo ascendendo
(Creatures back to
the creator)

circolo discendendo
(Creator-creature)
The higher loves
the lower

amore intrinseco
(God loves Himself)
The lower loves
the higher

prima materia
Chaos

Figure 9

ment. Such a relationship thus becomes a true anthropogony and a touchstone for testing the whole, conscious personality. Only now is it possible to understand the Ethics of Aristotle, according to which only what one strives for for one's own sake (for the sake of one's wholeness), suffices if life is to be bestowed with its highest value. Let us return once more to Plato, where he refers to Aristotle[197] on the subject of love: "the conjunction of man and woman is a begetting for both,"[198] because "the children of their union are fair and deathless."[199]

On the subject of marriage as the paradigm for human relationships, what can be deduced from the above observations from the psychological point of view is that it is the greatest, most exacting and most difficult demand that is made on us, but that it also offers us the greatest opportunity to become ourselves. The latter, of course, presupposes that there is *mutual* love, whether it be called Agape, Eros, Storge, Philia or Charity.[200] In other words it must correspond to the definition given to it by St. Paul in I Corinthians 13,[201] where, it must be noted, it is a gift of grace and is not something that we can create ourselves, even though we blithely talk of "making love."

As for the rewards of wholeness, it seems to us fitting to conclude, with a quotation from the Bible, as a Christian parallel, where the mystic Oneness relationship becomes particularly clear:

[197] Aristotle, Polit. II, 1262 b 16.
[198] Plato, Sympos. 206 C.
[199] Ibid. 209 C.
[200] Charitas Christi enim urget nor (II Cor. 5, 14).
[201] St. Paul, I Cor. 13.

I am the true vine, and my Father is the husbandman. Every branch in me that beareth not fruit, he taketh it away: and every branch that beareth fruit, he cleanseth it, that it may bear more fruit. Already ye are clean because of the word which I have spoken unto you. Abide in me, and I in you. As the branch cannot bear fruit of itself, except it abide in the vine; so neither can ye, except ye abide in me. I am the vine, ye are the branches: He that abideth in me and I in him, the same beareth much fruit: for apart from me ye can do nothing. If a man abide not in me, he is cast forth as a branch, and is withered; and they gather them, and cast them into the fire, and they are burned.[202]

---

[202] John 15, 1-6.

Epilogue

On completing this textbook, many a reader will go away with the impression that Jung is really old-fashioned. In fact the reader might have something there, but as psychologists we are not short of an explanation!

In discovering the collective unconscious, i.e., the *real* unconscious, Jung found himself having to deal with material which, because it was incomprehensible, had also been ignored. It was only through comparative studies of religion, myths, fairy tales, alchemy, and so on that these phenomena started to become understood for what they were, namely as statements of how this collective unconscious – the very soul of man – actually functioned. It was only then that there came into being a psychology truly worthy of the name "science of the soul." What emerged from this comparative approach to, and amplification of, the dream material of modern man, for example, was that the human psyche, when it comes to its basic functions, has been the same at all times and in all civilizations. In other words, the soul itself turns out to be very conservative. Whereas a few hundred years ago one might have dreamed about an eagle, today's dream might be about a jet plane. And if by any chance we should start to preen ourselves on our technical progress and totally ignore Icarus, this only proves that we not only no longer understand natural conditions, but in fact fondly imagine that we have outgrown them; and this is where the real danger of "modernism" lies. For this is the start of the vicious circle that leaves us blissfully unaware of the implications of our fascination with all things technological, so that we are inexorably caught in their clutches.

This may sound like the voice of doom, but it never occurs to anyone these days to study the Icarus myth or the mythology of the eagle, for Jung seems to have been the only one to recognize the therapeutic value of myths. He points us to this old and ancient material, which makes him conservative, too, for he is concerned with the old and ancient human soul, having demonstrated its constancy over the millennia. In the sphere of the living soul, however, nothing is antiquated. We should be thankful that amid all the confusion of our conscious reality there is at least one sphere of our inner selves that remains impregnable and is thus able to point to the future and to exert a healing influence.

"Ethos is man's fate"[203] is a perception worthy of the utmost veneration, and no amount of trendy psychological fads can offer any greater truth than this.

There is another way in which this perception makes us conservative, for when Ethos (our most essential being) is our destiny, then the starting point becomes the destination. I am indebted to David Roscoe at this point for drawing my attention to a relevant quotation from "Little Gidding" in T.S. Eliot's *The Four Quartets:*

> We shall not cease from exploration
> And the end of all our exploring
> Will be to arrive where we started
> And know the place for the first time.

Leone Ebreo's *circolo amoroso* should also be understood in this light, as well as the saying, "Become what you are." What we have tried to do is to draw up a plausible system for this perception on the basis of typology, for in terms of Jung's psychology this cycle traverses the compass of the four functions and two attitudes, which would correspond to the gaining of the *Quinta essentia.*

Gestaltung, Umgestaltung, Des ewigen Sinnes ewige Unterhaltung.

(Formation, Transformation, Eternal Mind's eternal recreation)
– Goethe, *Faust II*, I

---

[203] Heraclitus, Fr. B. 119.

Bibliography

Adler, A., *Study of Organ Inferiority and Its Psychical Compensation.* New York, 1917. German orig. 1907.

Adlerstein, A.M. und Irving, E.A., *The Relationship between Religious Belief and Negative Affect toward Death.* 66. Annual Convention of APA, Washington DC, 1958.

Aristotle, *Peri enhypniou* (On Dreaming).

— *Metaphysics 9.* 1074.

— *Nikomachean Ethics.*

— *'Peri tes kat' hypnon mantikes* (On Dream Interpretation).

Augustinus, *Confessiones.*

— *de vera religione.* IX, 16.

Avalon, A. (Sir John Woodroffe), *The Serpent Power.* Madras, 1918.

— *The Garland of Letters,* 3rd ed. Madras, 1955.

— *Shakti and Shakta: Essays and Addresses on the Sakta Tantrasastra.* German ed. 1962.

Bächtold-Stäubli, H. und Hoffmann-Krayer, E., *Handwörterbuch des deutschen Aberglaubens.* 10 Vols., Berlin, 1927-1942.

Balzac, H. de, *La peau de chagrin.* 1931.

Barlach, E., *Der tote Tag.* Berlin, 1925.

Bastian, A., *Der Völkergedanke im Aufbau einer Wissenschaft vom Menschen.* Berlin, 1881.

Baumann, U. / Angst, J. / Henne, A. / Muser, F.E., *Der Gray-Wheelwright-Test,* in: *Diagnostica,* XXI/2, p. 66-83, Göttingen, 1975.

Baynes, H.G., *Mythology of the Soul.* London, 1940.

Benoit, P., *L'Atlantide.* Paris, 1919.

Berthelot, M.P.E., *Collection des anciens alchimistes grecs.* Paris, 1888.

Boehringer, E., *Die Ausgrabungsarbeiten zu Pergamon im Jahre 1965.* (Archäologischer Anzeiger, 1966, Heft 4)

Bohr, N., *Atomic Theory and the Description of Nature.* New York, 1976. German orig. 1931

— *Licht und Leben.* In *Die Naturwissenschaften 21.* Berlin, 1933

Brhadaranyaka Upanishad.

Buchanan, S., *The Doctrine of Signatures*. London, 1938.

Burckhardt, G.E., *Gilgamesh*. Insel-Bücherei Nr. 203, Leipzig (no date).

Burckhardt, J., *Briefe*. Krit. bearbeitete Ausgabe von Max Burckhardt. Basel, 1955.

Byron, *The Pilgrimage of Childe Harold*. 1812.

Carus, C.G., *Psyche*. New York, 1970. German orig. 1846.

Chamisso, A. von, *Peter Schlemihls wundersame Geschichte*. 1814.

Chateaubriand, F.R., *Mémoires d'Outre-tombe*. Paris, 1848.

Cicero, *de divin*.

Clarke, E., and Dewhurst, K., *Illustrated History of Brain Function*, 1973.

Clemens Romanus. ep. in Romanos.

Colonna, F., *Hypnerotomachia Poliphili*. Venetiis, 1499.

Cook, A.B., *Zeus*. London 1940.

Corpus Hermeticum, ed. A.D. Nock und A.J. Festugière. Paris, 1960.

Corrie, J., *ABC of Jung's Psychology*. London, 1927.

Cuvier, G. de, *Le règne animale*. 8 vols. 1817.

Dante, *La divina commedia*.

Deußen, P., *Sechzig Upanishads des Veda* 3. Leipzig, 1921.

Dieterich, A., *Eine Mithrasliturgie*. Leipzig 1903,1966.

Dorneus, G., *Philosophia meditativa*, 1602.

DuBois-Reymond, E. *Reden,* Vol. 1 (Discourses).

Dunne, J.W., *An Experiment With Time*. London, 1927.

— *The Serial Universe*. London, 1934.

Ebreo, L., *Dialoghi d'Amore*. Roma 1535. Now ed. Carl Gebhardt (Bibliotheca Spinoziana, tome III), Heidelberg/London/Paris/Amsterdam, 1929.

Eddy, M.B., *Science and Health*. 16. 1875.

Emerson, R.W., *Essays* III. Halle (no date)

Empedokles, *Fragmenta*. in: Diels/Kranz, *Die Fragmente der Vorsokratiker* 6. Berlin, 1951.

Euhemeros, *Heilige Aufzeichnungen*.

Evangelium nach Thomas (The Gospel According to John). A. Guillaumont, ed. Leiden, 1959.

Evangelium Veritatis, in: *Codex Jung*, ed. M. Malinine, H.-Ch. Puech, G. Quispel. Zürich, 1956.

Fichte, J.G., *Vorlesungen über das Wesen des Gelehrten und seine Erscheinungen im Gebiete der Freiheit*. Berlin, 1806. In *Fichtes Werke,* 1971.

Ficino, Marsiio, *Commentarium in Convivium Platonis sive de amore*.

— *Theologia Platonica*.

Fico della Mirandola, *Heptaplus*.

Fierz-David, L., *The Dream of Poliphilo*. Spring, Dallas, 1987.

Flournoy, Th., *Des Indes à la planète Mars*. Paris/Genf, 1900.

Fludd, R., *Philosophia Moysaica*. Ghent, 1638.

Fraser, R., *The Flying Draper*. London, 1924. (The Traveller's Library, London 1931.)

Frazer, J.G., *The Golden Bough*, London, 1914.

Freud, S., *Psycho-Analytic Notes on an Autobiographical Account of a Case of Paranoia* (Dementia Paranoides). In Standard Edition, Vol XII, German orig. 1911.

— *Totem and Taboo*. 1913. SE XIII, Hogarth, London, 1991.

— *The Future of an Illusion*. SE XXI, Hogarth, London, 1991.

Freyd, M., *Introverts and Extraverts*. In *Psychol. Rev., 31*. Baltimore, 1924.

Furst, E., *Statistical Investigations on Word-Associations and on Familial Agreement in Reaction Type Among Uneducated Persons*, in *Studies in Word-Association*. C.G. Jung, ed., London, 1918. German orig. 1907.

Galton, F., *Hereditary Genius*. London, 1869.

Gillen, F.J. und Spencer, B., *The Native Tribes of Central Australia*. London, 1899.

Goethe, J.W., *Maxims and Reflections*.

— *Unterhaltungen deutscher Ausgewanderter*. Das Märchen.

— *Faust*.

— *Wilhelm Meisters theatralische Sendung*. First version.

— Nachgelassene Werke. *Zur Naturwissenschaft im Allgemeinen*.

Goetz, B., *Das Reich ohne Raum*. ca. 1920.

Govinda, Lama Anagarika, *Foundations of Tibetan Mysticism*. Weiser, York Beach, ME, 1969. German ed. 1972.

Green, C., *Out-Of-the-Body Experiences*. London, 1968.

Grimm, J., *Deutsche Mythologie* 4. Gütersloh, 1877. (reprint 1968/1969.)

Groß, O., *Die cerebrale Sekundärfunktion*. Leipzig, 1902.

— *Über psychopathische Minderwertigkeiten*. Leipzig, 1909.

Haggard, H.R., *She*. London, 1886.

Harding, E., *The Way of All Women*, London und New York, 1933.

Heine, H., *Zur Geschichte der Religion und Philosophie in Deutschland, II*. (Der Salon II). 1852.

Heraklit, *Fragmenta*.

Hodeilin, F., *Patmos*.

Hoffmann, E.T.A., *Die Elixiere des Teufels*. 1814.

— *Der goldne Topf*, 1815.

Hoffmann-Krayer, Ei. *Feste und Bräuche des Schweizervolkes*. Zürich, 1949.

Homer, *Iliad*.

Irving, E.A. und Adlerstein, A.M., *The Relationship between Religious Belief and Negative Affect toward Death*. 66. Annual Convention of APA, Washington D.C., 1958.

Jaffé, A., *Images and Symbols from E.T.A. Hoffmanns Märchen «Der goldne Topf»*, 4th edition, Daimon, Einsiedeln, 1990.
— *The Myth of Meaning*. Daimon, Einsiedeln, 1989. German orig. 1967.
— *Memories, Dreams, Reflections by C.G. Jung*, recorded and edited by Aniela Jaffé, New York, 1962.
James, W., *Principles of Psychology*. Harvard, 1890.
— *The Varieties of Religious Experience*. London, 1890.
Jantz, H., and Beringer, K., *Das Syndrom der Schwebeerlebnisses unmittelbar nach Kopfverletzungen*, in *Der Nervenarzt*, xvii. Berlin, 1944.
Jeans, J., *The Universe Around Us*. London, 1929.
Jordan, F., *Character as seen in Body and Parentage* 3. London, 1896.
Jung, C.G., *On the Psychology and Pathology of so-called Occult Phenomena*. In *Collected Works*, Vol. 1., German orig. 1902.
— *Symbols of Transformation*. In CW 5. (German orig. *Wandlungen und Symbole der Libido*, 1912).
— *The Content of the Psychoses*. In CW 3. German orig. 1914.
— *A Contribution to the Study of Psychological Types*. In CW 6. French orig. 1913.
— *On Psychological Understanding*. In *The Journal of Abnormal Psychology*, IX:6. Feb-Mar., 1915, now in CW 3.
— *Psychological Types*. In CW 6. German orig. 1921.
— *On Psychic Energy*. In CW 8. German orig. 1928.
— *The Psychology of the Transference*. In CW 16. German orig. 1946.
— *Über psychische Energetik und das Wesen der Träume*. Zurich, 1948.
— *Synchronicity: An Acausal Connecting Principle*. In CW 8. German orig. 1952.
— *Memories, Dreams, Reflections by C.G. Jung*, recorded and edited by Aniela Jaffé, New York, 1962.
Jung, C.G. und Wilhelm R., *The Secret of the Golden Flower*, with a European commentary by C.G. Jung, trans. Cary Baynes, London & NY 1931, new ed. 1962.
Jung, E., *Animus and Anima*. Dallas, various editions.
Kant, I., *Kritik der reinen Vernunft und Fortschritte der Metaphysik*. 1804.
Kantorowicz, E.H., *The King's Two Bodies. A Study in Medieaval Political Theology*. Princeton N.J., 1957.
Kemp, P., *Healing Ritual*. London, 1935.
Kerner, J., *Die Seherin von Prevorst*. Stuttgart and Tübingen, 1829.
Keyserling, H., *Südamerikanische Meditationen*. Stuttgart, 1932.
Kluger-Schärf, R., *The Archetypal Significance of Gilgamesh*. Daimon, Einsiedeln, 1991.
Knuchel, E.F., *Die Umwandlung in Kult, Magie und Rechtsbrauch*. Basel, 1919.

Komarius, *Buch des K., des Philosophen und Hohepriesters, der Cleopatra die göttliche und heilige Kunst des Steins der Philosophen lehrte*. Repr. Holland Press, London, 1963.

Koran, Sure 18, 64-81.

Koyré, A., *Études Galiléennes, À l'Aube de la Science Classique*. Paris, 1939.

Kretschmer, E., *Physique and Character* 1936. German orig., Leipzig, 1921.

Kristeller, P.O., *Eight Philosophers of the Italian Renaissance*. Stanford Calif.,1964.

Kubin, A., *Die andere Seite*. München, 1923.

Lagerlöf, S., *Gösta Berling*. 1891.

Lang, J.B. *Über Assoziationsversuche bei Schizophrenen und den Mitgliedern ihrer Familie*. Zurich diss., 1913.

Lao Tse, *Tao Te King*. 18. Übersetzt von R. Wilhelm: Das Buch des Alten vom Sinn und Leben. Jena, 1921.

Leonhard, B.K., *Die Gesetze des normalen Träumens*. Leipzig, 1939.

Leviticus.

Lévy-Bruhl, L., *Les fonctions-mentales dans les societés inférieures*. Paris, 1910.

Lhotsky, J., *Der Begriff «Prägung» in der vergleichend-analytischen Psychologie*. In *Beiträge zur Sexualforschung*, 6. Heft. Stuttgart, 1955.

Lichtenberg, G.Ch., *Vermischte Schriften*. Göttingen, 1844.

Lindner, R.M., *The Fifty-Minute Hour*. New York, 1955.

Linné, C. von, *Systema Naturae*. 1735.

— *Genera Plantarum*. 1737.

Lorenz, K., *Das sogenannte Böse*. Vienna, 1963.

Macrobius, *Commentariorum ex Cicerone in Somnium Scipionis*, libri duo.

Maier, M., *Scrutinium chymicum*. Frankfurt, 1687.

Maitland, E., *Anna Kingsford, Her Life, Letters, Diary and Work*, 2 vols. London, 1896.

Mann, H., *Prof. Unrat*. 1905.

Mehlich, R., *I.H. Fichtes Seelenlehre*. Zürich, 1935.

Meier, C.A., *Moderne Physik – Moderne Psychologie,* in *Die kulturelle Bedeutung der Komplexen Psychologie*. Berlin, 1935.

— *Healing Dream and Ritual.* Daimon Verlag, Einsiedeln, 1989. German orig. 1948.

— *The Unconscious in its Empirical Manifestations*. Sigo Press, Boston, 1984. German orig. 1968.

— *Dynamic Psychology and the Classical World*. In *Psychiatry and its History*. Mora and Brand, eds., Springfield, IL, 1970.

— *Individuation und psychologische Typen*. In *Zeitschr. f. Analyt. Psychol.*, I. Berlin, 1970.

— *Der Jungsche Gesichtspunk in der neueren experimentellen Schlaf- und Traumforschung.* In *Zeitschr. f. Analyt. Psychol.,* II. Berlin, 1971.

— *The Meaning and Significance of Dreams.* Boston: Sigo Press, 1987. German orig. 1972.

Meister Eckehart, *Schriften und Predigten.* Herman Bittner, ed., Jena, 1917.

Meyrink, G., *Des deutschen Spießers Wunderhorn.* München, 1913.

— *Der Golem.* 1915.

— *Das grüne Gesicht.* 1916.

— *Walpurgisnacht.* 1917.

— *Der Engel vom westlichen Fenster.* 1927.

Minucius Felix, *Octavius.*

Moffat, R., *Missionary Labors and Scenes in South Africa.* London, 1842.

Mookerjee, A., *Tantra Asana.* New York, 1975. German ed. 1971.

Musaem Hermeticum. *De sulphure.* Frankfurt, 1677.

Neumann, E., *The Great Mother,* Princeton, 1955.

Nietzsche, F., *The Birth of Tragedy.* German orig. *Die Geburt der Tragodie aus dem Geiste der Musik,* 1870/71.

— *Thus Spoke Zarathustra.* German orig. 1883/92.

Omar i Khajjam. *Rubaijat.*

Origen, *Leviticus Homily.*

Otto, R., *The Idea of the Holy.* (transl. John W. Harvey), New York, 1958.

Ovid, *Metamorphoses.*

Panizza, O., *Visionen der Dämmerung.* München, 1922.

Parmenides, *Fragmenta.* Diels/Kranz, *Die Fragmente der Vorsokratiker* 6, Berlin, 1951.

Patrizzi, F., Nova de universis philosophia. Venetiis, 1591.

Pauli, W., *Die philosophische Bedeutung der Idee der Komplementarität.* In *Experientia,* VI. Basel, 1950.

— *The Influence of Archetypal Ideas on the Scientific Ideas of Kepler.* In *The Interpretation of Nature and the Psyche,* New York, 1955.

— *Phanomen und physikalische Realitat.* In *Dialectica,* II. La Neueville, 1957.

Philo of Alexandria, *de opificio mundi.*

Plato, *Symposium.* Übersetzung Franz Boll. München, 1926.

— *Phaidros.*

— *Republic.*

— *Timaios.*

Plotin, *Enneaden,* IV. 3,8.

Prince, M., *The Dissociation of a Personality.* New York, 1905.

Purkinje, J.E., *Wachen, Schlafen, Traum und verwandte Zustände.* In *Handwörterbuch der Physiologie mit Rücksicht auf physiologische Pathologie,* Bd. III/2. Braunschweig, 1846.

Putscher, M., *Pneuma, Spiritus, Geist.* Wiesbaden, 1973.

Radin, R., *The Story of the American Indian.* New York, 1927.

Rasmussen, K., *Neue Menschen.* Bern, 1907.

Reitzenstein, R. und Schaeder H.H., *Studien zum antiken Synkretismus. Aus Iran und Griechenland.* Leipzig und Berlin, 1926.

Renusat, C.F.M. de, *Abelard.* Paris 1845. 2 Vols.

Rhine, L.E. und Rhine, J.B., *The Psychokinetic Effect.* Journ. of Paraps. VII. Durham NC, 1943.

Robert, F., *Thymèlé.* Paris, 1939.

Rosenkrantz, W., *Wissenschaft des Wissens und Begründung der besonderen Wissenschaften durch die allgemeine Wissenschaft.* Mainz, 1866.

Rouselle, E., *Seelische Führung im lebenden Taoismus?* In *Eranos-Jahrbuch 1933,* Zurich, 1934.

Rudolph, E., *Teufelsbündner im 20. Jh.,* in: Schweiz. Arch. f. Volkskunde. 72. Basel, 1976.

Schiller, F., *Spruch des Confucius,* Gedicht 183. 1799.

— *Die Piccolomini.*

— *On the Aesthetic Education of Man.* German orig. 1795.

— *On Naive and Sentimental Poetry.* German orig. 1795.

Schopenhauer, A., *Parerga I.*

— On the Fourfold Root of the Principle of Sufficient Reason.

Schott, A. und Soden, W. von, *Das Gilgamesch-Epos.* Reclam, Stuttgart, 1958.

Schreber, D.P., *Denkwürdigkeiten eines Nervenkranken.* Leipzig, 1903.

Schuré, E., *Les grands Initiés.* Paris, 1889.

— *Femmes inspiratrices et poétes annonciateurs.* Paris, 1907.

— *La prêtresse d'Isis 4.* Paris, 1927.

Servius, in Vergili Bucolica III, 77.

Shakespeare, *Othello.*

Shaw, G.B., *Pygmalion.* 1912.

Sophokles, *Antigone.*

Spitteler C.,*Prometheus und Epimetheus.* 1881.

— *Der olympische Frühling.* 1905.

— *Imago.* Jena 1906.

Stallmach, J., *Dynamis und Energeia.* Meisenheim am Glaan, 1959.

Stevenson, R.L., *The Strange Case of Dr. Jeckyll and Mr. Hyde.* 1886.

Stoeckli, A., *Die Visionen des seligen Bruder Klaus.* Einsiedeln, 1933.

Tertullian, *De testimonio animae, I.*

Uexküll, J. von, *Umwelt und Innenwelt der Tiere.* 2nd ed. Berlin, 1921.

— *Theoretische Biologie.* 2nd ed. Berlin, 1928.

Ungnad, A., *Die Religion der Babylonier und Assyrer.* Jena, 1921.

Vasadava, A.U., *Tripura Rahasya* (Jnanakanda). Varanasi,1965.

Vergil. *Aeneis.*

Verville, B. de, *Le songe de Poliphile*. Paris, 1926.

Vescher, F. Th., *Auch Einer*. 1879.

von den Steinen, K., *Unter den Naturvölkern Zentralbrasiliens*. Berlin, 1894.

Wells, H.G., *Christina Alberta's Father*. London (no date).

Werfel, F., *Spiegelmensch*. 1920.

Wickes, F.G., *Three Illustrations of the Power of the projected Image*, in: Studien zur Analytischen Psychologie C.G. Jungs I. Zürich, 1955.

Wilde, O., *The Picture of Dorian Gray*. 1891.

Wilhelm, R. (ed.), *I-Ging, Das Buch der Wandlungen*. Leipzig, 1924. Eugen Diederichs, Düsseldorf und Köln, 1974.

Wilhelm, R., *The Secret of the Golden Flower*, with a European commentary by C.G. Jung, trans. Cary Baynes, London & NY 1931, new ed. 1962.

Winthuis, J., *Das Zweigeschlechterwesen bei den Zentralaustraliern und anderen Völkern*. Leipzig, 1928.

Wolff, T., *Studien zu C.G. Jungs Psychologie*. Zürich, 1981 (English language translation in preparation).

Zimmer, H., *Kunstform und Yoga im indischen Kultbild*. Berlin, 1926.

— *Maya, der indische Mythos*. Stuttgart, 1936.

I should like to add that a typological test has recently been developed by Mary Loomis and June Singer. A preliminary publication is entitled *The Singer-Loomis Inventory of Personality: A Measure of Cognitive Styles Based on C.G. Jung's Theory of Psychological Types*. There also exists a brief publication entitled, *About the SLIP: A Preliminary Manual for the Singer-Loomis Inventory of Personality*. Both works are dated 1979.

Index

ENGLISH PUBLICATIONS BY *DAIMON*

Susan Bach – *Life Paints its Own Span*
E.A. Bennet – *Meetings with Jung*
George Czuczka – *Imprints of the Future*
Heinrich Karl Fierz – *Jungian Psychiatry*
von Franz / Frey-Rohn / Jaffé – *What is Death?*
Liliane Frey-Rohn – *Friedrich Nietzsche*
Yael Haft – *Hands: Archetypal Chirology*
Siegmund Hurwitz – *Lilith, the first Eve*
Aniela Jaffé   – *The Myth of Meaning*
                    – *Was C.G. Jung a Mystic?*
                    – *From the Life und Work of C.G. Jung*
                    – *Death Dreams and Ghosts*
Verena Kast   – *A Time to Mourn*
                    – *Sisyphus*
James Kirsch   – *The Reluctant Prophet*
Rivkah Schärf Kluger   – *The Gilgamesh Epic*
Rafael López-Pedraza   – *Hermes and his Children*
                    – *Cultural Anxiety*
Alan McGlashan – *The Savage and Beautiful Country*
                    – *Gravity and Levity: The Philosophy of Paradox*
Gitta Mallasz (Transcription) – *Talking with Angels*
C.A. Meier   – *Healing Dream and Ritual*
                    – *A Testament to the Wilderness*
Laurens van der Post – *A «Festschrift»*
R.M. Rilke – *Duino Elegies*
Susan Tiberghien – *Looking for Gold: A Year in Jungian Analysis*
Ann Ulanov – *The Wizards' Gate*

Jungian Congress Papers:
Jerusalem 1983 – *Symbolic and Clinical Approaches*
Berlin 1986 – *Archetype of Shadow in a Split World*
Paris 1989 – *Dynamics in Relationship*
Chicago 1992 – *The Transcendent Function*

Available from your bookstore or from our distributors:

In the United States: *In Great Britain:*

Atrium Publishers Group   Chiron Publications   Airlift Book Company
P.O. Box 108   400 Linden Avenue   26-28 Eden Grove
Lower Lake, CA 95457   Wilmette, IL 60091   London N7 8EF, England
Tel. (707) 995 3906   Tel. (708) 256 7551   Tel. (607) 5792 and 5798
Fax: (707) 995 1814   Fax: (708) 256 2202   Fax (607) 6714

Worldwide: Daimon Verlag
                    Hauptstrasse 85
                    CH-8840 Einsiedeln Switzerland
                    Tel. (41)(55) 532266
                    Fax (41)(55) 532231   *Write for our complete catalog!*